SIMPLE THINGS OF LIFE

THE HIDDEN KEY TO HAPPINESS

ANKIT MISHRA

Made with ♥ on the Notion Press Platform
www.notionpress.com

Dedicated to my loving wife who inspired me to embark on a journey of writing my thoughts in a notebook, and now, that very notebook has transformed into my debut book.

Contents

Contents

About The Author

Ankit Mishra is a mechanical engineer based in Pune, India. He currently works for an automotive multinational Company, alongside his engineering career, Ankit has always had a passion for reading books.

Inspired by his love for books and the profound impact they have had on his life, Ankit decided to venture into writing himself. "Simple Things of Life" marks his debut as an author, showcasing his unique perspective on the beauty and significance of everyday moments.

His writing style captures the essence of simplicity, emphasizing the often-overlooked aspects of life that bring joy, meaning, and contentment. Through his book, he encourages readers to slow down, appreciate the present, and find happiness in the simple pleasures that surround them.

As a mechanical engineer, Ankit's acute observation skills and attention to detail translate seamlessly into his writing. His ability to extract profound insights from seemingly ordinary occurrences makes "Simple Things of Life" a delightful and thought-provoking read.

Ankit resides in Pune, where he finds solace in the serene surroundings and draws inspiration from the vibrant city life. When he is not engrossed in writing or working on engineering projects, he can be found exploring local bookstores, immersing himself in the worlds created by other authors, and seeking inspiration for his next literary endeavour.

"Simple Things of Life" is Ankit's first published book, and he hopes that readers will connect with its themes, reflect on their own lives, and rediscover the beauty in the simplicity that surrounds us all.

Contact Information:
Email: er.ankit08@gmail.com
Instagram: @ankit.mishra19
Facebook: www.facebook.com/ankit.mishra.1908
LinkedIn: www.linkedin.com/in/ankitmishra19/

Acknowledgements

I would like to express my heartfelt gratitude to the individuals who have played an instrumental role in the creation of this book, which marks a significant milestone in my life. Their unwavering support, love, and guidance have been invaluable throughout this journey.

First and foremost, I am eternally grateful to **My Beloved Wife**. Your unwavering belief in me and your unconditional love have been my anchor during the challenging times. Your patience, understanding, and constant encouragement have fueled my determination to pursue this endeavor. Thank you for standing by my side and for being my unwavering source of inspiration.

I would also like to extend my deepest appreciation to **My Parents**. Your endless support, sacrifices, and tireless dedication have molded me into the person I am today. Your belief in my abilities has been the driving force behind my pursuit of this book. Thank you for instilling in me the values of perseverance, resilience, and the importance of always striving for greatness.

Additionally, I am indebted to my college professor **M.K. Jain Sir**, whose teachings and mentorship have left an indelible impact on my life. Your wisdom, guidance, your values, and passion for knowledge have ignited a fire within me to continuously explore and grow. Your unwavering faith in my potential has pushed me to surpass my own limitations. Thank you for your invaluable lessons, insightful feedback, and for nurturing my intellectual curiosity.

To all my friends, family, and loved ones who have offered their unwavering support, encouragement, and patience, I am deeply grateful. Your belief in me, countless conversations, and words of encouragement have provided the fuel necessary to complete this book. Your presence in my life has been a constant reminder of the importance of community and the power of human connections.

Lastly, I would like to express my gratitude to the readers of this book. It is for you that these words have been penned. I hope that my experiences, insights, and lessons shared within these pages will serve as a guiding light on your own journey towards personal growth and fulfillment.

With profound appreciation and heartfelt gratitude,

Ankit Mishra

CHAPTER ONE

Introduction: Defining the "Simple things"

In our fast-paced and ever-changing world, it is easy to get caught up in the pursuit of more - more money, more success, more possessions, more experiences. We are told that these are the things that will bring us happiness and fulfilment in life. Being successful and wealthy is definitely not wrong, but what if the key to happiness and success was actually much simpler than we thought? What if the actual happiness lies in small things that our society never teaches us?

In a world that often glorifies complexity and constant progress, we usually overlook the beauty and importance of simple things. We are too busy in our job or business to ignore and never pay attention to the magic of simple things in our life. Simple things in life are the things that bring us joy, peace, and fulfilment without requiring us to jump through hoops or attain a certain level of success. This teaches us to being happy in the journey of success. They are the things that remind us of the magic in everyday life and the power of the present moment. These simple things can be anything from a warm cup of tea on a chilly day, to a kind word from a friend, to a beautiful sunset over the ocean. They may seem insignificant, but they have the ability to ground us, remind us of what is truly important, and help us navigate the ups and downs of life.

But why do we overlook these simple things? Why do we think that more is always better? Part of it may be cultural - we are conditioned to believe that success and happiness are synonymous with material wealth and status. The race or competition starts from schooling and never ends. Our tendency to compare with someone at better position. Part of it may also be human nature - we are wired to seek out new experiences, which can make us overlook the familiar and ordinary. and these simple things are defiantly from our routine which appears to be ordinary and we simply overlook it.

However, the truth is that simple things in life are often the most profound. They have the power to connect us with ourselves, with others, and with the world around us. They can help us cultivate gratitude, kindness, and compassion, which are essential qualities for success and happiness in life.

Simplicity can be a powerful tool for success in both our personal and professional lives. In our personal lives, simplifying our daily routines and focusing on the things that truly matter can help us reduce stress and find more time for the things we love. By cutting out unnecessary activities or possessions, we can create more space for the things that bring us joy and fulfilment.

In our professional lives, simplicity can also be a key factor in success. By simplifying our goals and focusing on the most important tasks, we can increase our productivity and achieve greater results. In addition, simplifying our communication and avoiding unnecessary complexity can help us connect more effectively with others and build stronger relationships.

Of course, it is important to acknowledge that simplicity is not always easy to achieve in a world that often encourages complexity and excess. However, by making a conscious effort to simplify our lives and focus on the things that truly matter, we can unlock the power of simplicity and find greater happiness and success in all areas of our lives.

Simple things can differ from person to person, but they share a few common characteristics. They are things that:

- Bring us joy:

Simple things are things that bring us joy and happiness, regardless of how big or small they are. They are the things that make us smile, laugh, or feel content, such as a warm cup of tea, a good book, or a walk-in nature.

- Ground us in the present:

Simple things are things that help us stay present in the moment and appreciate what we have right now. They are the things that remind us to slow down, breathe, and enjoy the simple pleasures in life, such as the taste of our favourite food or the sound of our loved ones' voices.

- Are accessible to everyone:

Simple things are things that are accessible to everyone, regardless of their background, income, or social status. They are the things that anyone can enjoy, such as a sunset, a kind word, or a hug from a loved one.

- Are free or inexpensive:

Simple things are things that do not require a lot of money or resources to enjoy. They are the things that can be found in nature, created by our own hands, or experienced with the people we love, such as a homemade meal, a picnic in the park, or a game of catch.

simple things in life can often be the most valuable. By embracing simplicity and focusing on the things that truly matter, we can find greater joy, peace, and success in our personal and professional lives. So, take a moment to appreciate the simple things in your life, and see how they can make a big impact.

In this book, we will explore the power of simple things in life, and how they can make us happier and more successful in both our personal and professional lives. We will also provide practical tips and exercises for cultivating gratitude, mindfulness, and other qualities that can help us appreciate and embrace simple things in life. So, if you are ready to discover the power of simple things, let's begin!

CHAPTER TWO

Gratitude: Finding Joy in the Present Moment

In today's fast-paced world, it is easy to get caught up in the hustle and bustle of life, always looking towards the future and what is next on the to-do list. However, we often forget to take a step back and appreciate the present moment. Gratitude is the act of being thankful for what we have in our lives, and it can help us find joy and contentment in the present moment. Gratitude is a powerful tool that can help us appreciate the simple things in our lives, and it can lead to greater happiness and success. In this chapter, we will explore the importance of gratitude and how we can cultivate it in our lives.

Gratitude is a powerful emotion that has been linked to a range of benefits, including improved mental health, better relationships, and increased resilience. When we take the time to acknowledge the things, we are grateful for, we shift our focus from what we don't have to what we do have, and this can have a profound impact on our well-being.

One of the simplest ways to cultivate gratitude is to keep a gratitude journal. Each day, take a few minutes to reflect on the things you are thankful for and write them down. It can be as simple as being grateful for a good cup of coffee or a warm bed to sleep in, or it could be something more profound, like the love and support of family and friends. By focusing on the positive aspects of your life, you will begin to notice that there is always something to be grateful for, no matter how small.

Another way to cultivate gratitude is to practice mindfulness. Mindfulness is the act of being present in the moment, without judgment or distraction. By taking the time to focus on the present moment, you can learn to appreciate the beauty and wonder of the world around you. Whether it is a stunning sunset or the laughter of children playing in the park, there is always something to be grateful for in the present moment. We will discuss more about mindfulness in coming chapter.

Gratitude can also help us navigate difficult times in our lives. When we are facing challenges, it's easy to get caught up in negative thinking and worry. However, by focusing on the things we are grateful for, we can shift our perspective and find hope and positivity in even the toughest of situations.

Gratitude is defined as the quality of being thankful and showing appreciation for the good things in our lives. It is an attitude of recognizing and acknowledging the positive aspects of our lives, regardless of how small they may seem. When we practice gratitude regularly, we tend to experience more positive emotions, such as joy, love, and contentment. Additionally, gratitude has been linked to improved physical and mental health, stronger relationships, and greater resilience in the face of adversity.

In our fast-paced lives, it can be easy to overlook the small things that bring us joy and make our lives better. We may take for granted the roof over our heads, the food on our table, or the people who love us. However, when we take the time to appreciate these simple things, we begin to see the world in a more positive light. We begin to realize that we have more than we need, and that our lives are filled with blessings that we may have otherwise missed.

here are some scientific research studies that demonstrate the benefits of gratitude:

- In a study published in the Journal of Personality and Social Psychology in 2003, researchers found that participants who wrote down things they were grateful for each week had higher levels of optimism, felt better about their lives, and exercised more than those who didn't.
- Another study, published in the Journal of Happiness Studies in 2013, found that people who practiced gratitude had better sleep quality and felt less tired during the day.
- A study published in the Journal of Positive Psychology in 2014 found that participants who expressed gratitude toward their partners had stronger and more positive relationships.
- In a study published in the Journal of Personality and Social Psychology in 2015, researchers found that gratitude was associated with better mental health, including less depression and anxiety.
- A study published in the journal Emotion in 2016 found that people who practiced gratitude had higher levels of activity in the hypothalamus, a brain region involved in stress and anxiety regulation.

These studies show that practicing gratitude can have significant benefits for our mental and physical well-being, as well as our relationships.

Why Gratitude Matters

Gratitude is the practice of recognizing and appreciating the good things in your life. It is easy to get caught up in the stresses and challenges of daily life and overlook the blessings that surround us. But when we take the time to express gratitude, we shift our focus from what is lacking to what is abundant. Gratitude can help us to:

- Cultivate Positive Emotions:

When we focus on what we are grateful for, we experience positive emotions such as joy, contentment, and peace. These emotions help us to feel more resilient and better equipped to handle life's challenges.

- Build Stronger Relationships:

When we express gratitude to others, we strengthen our connections and build trust. Gratitude can help us to feel more connected and supported, which is essential for our well-being.

- Improve Our Physical Health:

Gratitude has been shown to have physical benefits such as better sleep, lower blood pressure, and reduced symptoms of depression.

Here are a few ways to cultivate gratitude for the smallest things in life:

- Keep a Gratitude Journal

One of the most effective ways to cultivate gratitude is to keep a gratitude journal. Each day, write down three things you are grateful for, no matter how small or insignificant they may seem. This simple exercise will help you focus on the positive things in your life and develop a habit of gratitude.

- Express Gratitude to Others

Expressing gratitude to others is a powerful way to cultivate gratitude in yourself and others. Make a habit of thanking the people in your life for the things they do, whether it's a kind word, a thoughtful gesture, or simply being there for you. Expressing gratitude toward your life-partner can strengthen the bond. Be thankful for friends who supported in your hard times.

- Practice Mindfulness

Practicing mindfulness can help you cultivate gratitude by bringing your attention to the present moment and appreciating the beauty and richness of your experiences. Take a few minutes each day to sit in silence, focusing on your breath and the sensations in your body.

- Use Positive Affirmations

Positive affirmations can help you shift your mindset and cultivate gratitude. Write down positive statements about yourself, your life, and your experiences, and repeat them to yourself throughout the day.

- Volunteer or Donate

Volunteering or donating to a cause you care about can help you cultivate gratitude by giving back to others and recognizing the privileges you have. Find a cause that resonates with you and get involved in any way you can.

- Practice Gratitude Meditation

Gratitude meditation involves focusing on things you are grateful for and letting that feeling fill your body and mind. Find a quiet place to sit, close your eyes, and focus on the feeling of gratitude.

- Practice Forgiveness

Forgiveness is an essential aspect of cultivating gratitude. Let go of grudges and resentments, and focus on the positive aspects of the situation.

- Practice Self-Care

Taking care of yourself is a crucial part of cultivating gratitude. Make time for activities that bring you joy, such as exercise, reading, or spending time with loved ones.

- Keep a Gratitude Jar

A gratitude jar is a fun and creative way to cultivate gratitude. Each day, write down something you are grateful for on a piece of paper and put it in the jar. Whenever you need a pick-me-up, read through the notes and be reminded of all the good in your life.

- Practice Gratitude in the Moment

Take a moment each day to pause and appreciate the beauty around you. Whether it's the colors of the sunset, the taste of your favorite food, or the sound of a loved one's voice, focus on the present moment and express gratitude for it.

- Surround Yourself with Positive People

Surrounding yourself with positive, uplifting people can help you cultivate gratitude by creating a supportive environment. Seek out people who inspire you and bring out the best in you.

- Read Inspirational Quotes

Reading inspirational quotes can help you shift your perspective and cultivate gratitude. Find quotes that resonate with you and display them in places where you can see them regularly.

- Practice Gratitude in Challenging Times

Practicing gratitude in challenging times can help you find meaning and perspective in difficult situations. Instead of focusing on the negative, look for the silver linings and express gratitude for the lessons you are learning and the opportunities for growth.

- Create a Gratitude Ritual

Creating a gratitude ritual can help you make gratitude a regular part of your daily routine. This can be anything from saying a prayer of gratitude before meals to writing a thank you note to someone each week.

- Practice Gratitude with Your Senses

Using your senses to cultivate gratitude can be a powerful way to connect with the present moment and appreciate the world around you. Take a moment each day to savor the taste of your food, feel the warmth of the sun on your skin, or listen to the sound of a bird singing.

cultivating gratitude is a simple but powerful way to improve your mental and emotional well-being and create a more fulfilling life. By incorporating these 15 steps into your daily routine, you can develop a habit of gratitude and reap the many benefits it brings. Remember to be patient and persistent, and trust that the practice of gratitude will bring positivity and abundance into your life.

gratitude is a so powerful that it can help us find joy and contentment in the present moment. By focusing on the things, we are thankful for, we can shift our perspective and cultivate a sense of happiness and well-being. So, take a moment each day to reflect on the things you are grateful for, and learn to appreciate the beauty and wonder of the world around you.

I would recommend to read three books, The Secret, The Magic and The Power, written by Rhonda Byrne, or watch her documentary named The Secret, which is available on YouTube.

CHAPTER THREE

Kindness - The Power of Small Acts

In a world where we are constantly bombarded with negative news and messages, it is easy to become cynical and jaded. However, one of the simplest and most powerful ways to counteract this negativity is through acts of kindness. Kindness, no matter how small, has the power to transform both the giver and the receiver. In this chapter, we will explore the many benefits of kindness and how it can be incorporated into our daily lives.

What is Kindness?

Kindness is the act of being friendly, generous, and considerate towards others. It can take many forms, from a simple smile or a kind word to a more significant act of generosity or compassion. The key is that kindness is an intentional act, something that is done with the purpose of making someone else's day a little brighter.

The Benefits of Kindness

There are many benefits to practicing kindness, both for the giver and the receiver. Some of these benefits include:

- Improved mental health:

Studies have shown that acts of kindness can boost our mood and reduce stress levels. When we do something kind for someone else, it activates the reward centres in our brain, releasing dopamine and other feel-good chemicals.

- Increased empathy:

When we practice kindness, we become more attuned to the needs and feelings of others. This can lead to increased empathy and a greater ability to connect with those around us.

- Strengthened relationships:

Kindness can help to build and strengthen relationships, whether it's with friends, family, or co-workers. When we show kindness to others, they are more likely to reciprocate, creating a positive feedback loop.

- Improved physical health:

Studies have also shown that acts of kindness can have a positive impact on our physical health. For example, one study found that people who performed acts of kindness had lower levels of inflammation in their bodies, which has been linked to a range of health problems.

Small Acts of Kindness

While grand gestures of kindness can be powerful, it's often the small acts that make the most significant impact. Here are a few examples of small acts of kindness that can make a big difference:

- Smile at someone:

A smile can go a long way towards brightening someone's day. Whether it's a stranger on the street or a co-worker in the office, taking a moment to smile and acknowledge someone can make them feel seen and valued.

- Hold the door open:

This simple act of courtesy can make a big difference, particularly for someone who may be carrying a heavy load or struggling with mobility.

- Send a kind message:

Whether it's a text, an email, or a handwritten note, taking the time to send a kind message to someone can make their day. It can be as simple as telling them you appreciate them or thanking them for something they've done.

- Buy someone a coffee:

The next time you're in line at a coffee shop, consider buying a coffee for the person behind you. It's a small act, but it can be a lovely surprise for someone who may be having a rough day.

Incorporating Kindness into Daily Life

Incorporating kindness into our daily lives is easier than we might think. Here are a few tips to help make kindness a habit:

- Start small:

Begin by incorporating one small act of kindness into your day, such as holding the door open for someone or sending a kind message to a friend.

- Be mindful:

Pay attention to the people around you and look for opportunities to show kindness. It could be as simple as noticing when someone looks sad and offering a kind word.

- Practice gratitude:

Cultivating a sense of gratitude can help us to be more mindful of the kindnesses we receive from others and inspire us to pay it forward. Take a few moments each day to reflect on the people and things in your life that you are grateful for.

- Set reminders:

If you find it challenging to remember to practice kindness, consider setting reminders for yourself. You could write a note and leave it on your desk or set a reminder on your phone.

- Get involved in volunteer work:

Volunteering is an excellent way to practice kindness on a larger scale. Look for local volunteer opportunities in your community, whether it's helping out at a food bank or a shelter.

- Practice self-kindness:

Kindness towards oneself is just as important as kindness towards others. Take time each day to do something kind for yourself, whether it's taking a relaxing bath or treating yourself to your favourite food.

The Power of Small Acts

It's easy to feel overwhelmed by the problems of the world and to believe that we can't make a significant difference. However, as we have seen, small acts of kindness can have a powerful impact. By showing kindness towards others, we can create a ripple effect, spreading positivity and compassion throughout our communities.

Moreover, the act of kindness has a positive impact not only on the receiver but also on the giver. When we practice kindness, we are reminded of our interconnectedness and our capacity to make a positive difference in the world. Kindness can help to boost our mood, reduce stress levels, and increase our overall sense of wellbeing.

In conclusion, kindness is a powerful force that has the potential to transform both our individual lives and our communities. By incorporating small acts of kindness into our daily lives, we can create a more compassionate, empathetic, and positive world. As the writer Aesop once said, "**No act of kindness, no matter how small, is ever wasted.**" So, let's take a moment each day to practice kindness towards others and towards ourselves and make the world a better place, one small act at a time.

CHAPTER FOUR

Mindfulness: Being Fully Present

Have you ever found yourself going through the motions of life without actually being present in the moment? Maybe you're eating a meal while scrolling through social media or having a conversation with someone while thinking about something else entirely. We've all been there, but it's important to recognize that this kind of distracted living can rob us of joy, fulfillment, and success. That's why practicing mindfulness, or being fully present in the moment, is crucial to living a happy and successful life.

What is Mindfulness?

At its core, mindfulness is simply the act of paying attention to the present moment with curiosity and without judgment. It's about being fully engaged in the present moment, without letting our thoughts and emotions distract us from what's happening right in front of us. Mindfulness can be practiced in many different ways, but all of them involve intentionally focusing your attention on what you're doing, thinking, or feeling.

Benefits of Mindfulness

There are countless benefits to practicing mindfulness, both for our personal and professional lives. Here are just a few of the many ways that mindfulness can improve our well-being and success:

- Reduced Stress:

Mindfulness has been shown to reduce stress and anxiety, both of which can have negative impacts on our physical and mental health.

- Improved Focus:

When we're fully present in the moment, we're better able to focus on the task at hand, which can help us be more productive and successful.

- Better Relationships:

Mindfulness can help us be more attentive and empathetic in our relationships, leading to stronger connections and better communication.

- Increased Creativity:

Being fully present and engaged in the present moment can help us tap into our creative potential and come up with new and innovative ideas.

- Improved Mental Health:

Mindfulness has been shown to improve a variety of mental health conditions, including depression, anxiety, and PTSD.

How to Practice Mindfulness

There are many different ways to practice mindfulness, and what works for one person may not work for another. However, here are some simple techniques to get you started:

- Mindful Breathing:

Take a few moments to focus on your breath, inhaling and exhaling deeply and slowly. Whenever your mind starts to wander, gently bring your attention back to your breath. this simple activity is very powerful and effective.

- Body Scan:

Close your eyes and scan your body from head to toe, noticing any sensations or feelings that arise. Don't judge or try to change anything, just observe.

- Mindful Eating:

Take a few minutes to really savor and enjoy your food, paying attention to its taste, texture, and aroma.

- Walking Meditation:

Go for a walk and focus your attention on the physical sensations of your body moving, as well as the sights, sounds, and smells around you.

- Mindful Listening:

The next time you're having a conversation, really listen to the other person without interrupting or getting distracted by your own thoughts. active listening is a critical skills to develop but very useful in person and professional life.

Incorporating Mindfulness into Your Daily Life

Practicing mindfulness doesn't have to be a separate activity that you only do for a few minutes each day. Instead, try to incorporate mindfulness into your daily routines and activities. Here are some examples:

- Mindful Morning Routine:

Instead of rushing through your morning routine, take a few moments to really savor your coffee or tea, stretch your body, and set intentions for the day ahead.

- Mindful Work:

Instead of multitasking and trying to do everything at once, focus on one task at a time and give it your full attention. Take breaks throughout the day to stretch, breathe deeply, and clear your mind.

- Mindful Eating:

Instead of mindlessly snacking throughout the day, take a few moments to really savor and enjoy your food. Eat slowly, chew your food well, and pay attention to its taste, texture, and aroma.

- Mindful Exercise:

Instead of going through the motions at the gym or on a run, focus on the physical sensations of your body moving. Notice your breathing, the feel of your muscles working, and the rhythm of your movement.

- Mindful Relationships:

When spending time with loved ones, make an effort to really be present with them. Put your phone away, make eye contact, and actively listen to what they have to say.

Practicing mindfulness is a simple yet powerful way to improve our overall well-being and success. By being fully present in the moment, we can reduce stress, improve focus, strengthen relationships, tap into our creativity, and enhance our mental health. With so many benefits, it's no wonder that mindfulness has become such a popular practice in recent years. So, the next time you find yourself distracted or stressed out, take a few moments to practice mindfulness and be fully present in the moment. Your mind and body will thank you for it.

CHAPTER FIVE

Connection: The Importance of Relationships

In today's world, where technology has made communication easier than ever before, it's ironic that many people feel more disconnected from others than ever before. Social media platforms and instant messaging services have created a superficial sense of connection, but they often lack the depth and quality of real human relationships.

In this chapter, we'll explore the importance of connection and relationships in our lives. We'll discuss how they contribute to our happiness and success, and why investing time and energy in building strong relationships is one of simple things we can do to improve our lives.

Human beings are social animals. We crave connection, interaction, and community. We all need other people in our lives to feel fulfilled, happy, and successful. It is said that no man is an island, and this is especially true when it comes to relationships.

The Power of Connection

Relationships come in many different forms - family, friends, coworkers, romantic partners, and acquaintances. Regardless of the type of relationship, the power of connection remains the same. Relationships allow us to feel seen, heard, and valued. They provide us with a sense of belonging and identity.

When we feel connected to others, we are more likely to experience positive emotions such as joy, contentment, and love. We also tend to have better physical health, lower levels of stress, and longer life spans. In fact, research has shown that social isolation and loneliness can be just as harmful to our health as smoking, obesity, and lack of exercise.

The Science of Connection

From a scientific perspective, human beings are social creatures. We are wired to connect with others, to form social bonds, and to rely on each other for survival. Research has shown that strong relationships and social support networks are associated with a range of health benefits, including reduced stress, lower blood pressure, and a stronger immune system.

But it's not just physical health that benefits from social connections. Our mental health and emotional wellbeing are also closely linked to the quality of our relationships. Studies have shown that people with strong social networks are less likely to experience depression, anxiety, and loneliness. They also tend to have higher self-esteem and greater resilience in the face of adversity.

The Importance of Authentic Relationships

When we talk about the importance of relationships, it's important to clarify what we mean by "relationships." Not all relationships are created equal, and not all of them are equally beneficial.

For example, superficial relationships based on shared interests or hobbies may provide some enjoyment or entertainment, but they don't necessarily provide the deep sense of connection and belonging that we need to thrive. Similarly, relationships based solely on transactional exchanges (e.g., networking for professional gain) may be helpful in achieving specific goals, but they don't necessarily lead to lasting, meaningful connections.

Authentic relationships, on the other hand, are based on mutual trust, respect, and genuine caring. They involve vulnerability, empathy, and emotional intimacy. Authentic relationships provide us with a sense of belonging, acceptance, and support, which can help us navigate life's challenges and achieve our goals.

The Benefits of Strong Relationships

Strong relationships offer a range of benefits that can enhance our lives in many ways. Here are just a few examples:

- Improved mental health:

As mentioned earlier, strong social connections are associated with reduced risk of depression, anxiety, and other mental health issues.

- Increased resilience:

When we have a strong support network, we're better able to cope with stress, trauma, and other challenges that life may throw our way.

- Greater happiness:

Studies have consistently shown that people with strong social connections report higher levels of happiness and life satisfaction.

- Professional success:

Strong relationships can be an asset in the workplace, providing opportunities for networking, mentorship, and collaboration.

- Longer lifespan:

Research has shown that people with strong social connections tend to live longer than those who are socially isolated.

Connection in Personal Life

In our personal lives, relationships are essential for our emotional and mental well-being. The people we choose to surround ourselves with can have a significant impact on our happiness and overall quality of life. Positive relationships provide us with a support system, allowing us to share our experiences and emotions with others.

Having healthy relationships can also help us navigate life's challenges. When we face difficult times, having people we can rely on can make all the difference. They can offer us comfort, advice, and perspective, helping us to make sense of our experiences and find meaning in them.

Relationships help us to grow and develop as individuals. Our interactions with others can teach us valuable lessons about empathy, communication, and self-awareness. We can also learn from their experiences and perspectives, broadening our own understanding of the world.

Connection in Professional Life

Relationships are just as important in our professional lives. The people we work with can impact our job satisfaction, performance, and career advancement. Positive relationships at work can create a sense of community and belonging, leading to increased motivation and productivity.

Having strong professional relationships can also help us to advance in our careers. Networking and building relationships with others in our industry can lead to new opportunities and career growth. We can learn from their experiences, receive valuable feedback, and gain access to resources and information that can help us succeed.

Relationships can help us to build trust and establish a positive reputation. When we have strong relationships with coworkers, clients, and customers, we are more likely to be viewed as reliable, trustworthy, and competent. This can lead to increased job satisfaction, higher salaries, and more fulfilling career paths.

Building and Maintaining Relationships

While relationships are essential, they also require effort and investment. Building and maintaining positive relationships requires time, attention, and care. Here are some tips for building and maintaining strong relationships:

- Be intentional:

Building strong relationships takes time and effort. Be intentional about cultivating new relationships and nurturing existing ones.

- Listen actively:

Good communication is the foundation of any strong relationship. Practice active listening and make an effort to understand others' perspectives.

- Show empathy:

Empathy is the ability to understand and share the feelings of others. It's a key ingredient in building strong, authentic relationships.

- Be vulnerable:

Authentic relationships require vulnerability. Be willing to share your own thoughts, feelings, fears, and experiences with others.

- Practice gratitude:

Expressing gratitude for the people in our lives can help strengthen our relationships and enhance our sense of connection.

- Be present:

When you are with someone, be fully present and engaged. Put away your phone, make eye contact, and actively listen to what they have to say.

- Communicate effectively:

Effective communication is key to building strong relationships. Be clear and direct in your communication, and be willing to listen to others' perspectives.

- Show appreciation:

Take the time to show appreciation for the people in your life. Express gratitude for their support, encouragement, and kindness.

- Be reliable:

Follow through on your commitments and be dependable. This builds trust and helps to establish a positive reputation.

- Be open-minded:

Be open to new experiences, perspectives, and ideas. This can lead to growth and a deeper understanding of yourself and others.

CHAPTER SIX

Nature: The Healing Power of the Outdoors

We spend so much time indoors, sitting at desks, staring at screens, and rushing from one task to the next. It's no wonder that so many of us feel stressed, anxious, and disconnected. But there's a simple solution to this problem: spending time in nature.

Nature has a way of calming our minds, soothing our souls, and rejuvenating our spirits. It reminds us of the beauty and wonder of the world, and helps us reconnect with our inner selves. Whether we're hiking through the woods, walking along a beach, or simply sitting in a park, nature has the power to heal us in profound ways.

One of the reasons that nature is so healing is that it offers a respite from the constant stimulation of modern life. In nature, we can unplug from our devices, quiet our minds, and focus on the present moment. We can breathe in fresh air, listen to the sounds of birds singing and leaves rustling, and feel the warmth of the sun on our skin. We can let go of our worries and distractions, and simply be.

Studies have shown that spending time in nature can have a host of physical and mental health benefits. For example, research has found that spending time in green spaces can lower our stress levels, reduce symptoms of depression and anxiety, and even boost our immune systems. Other studies have shown that being in nature can improve our cognitive function, enhance our creativity, and increase our feelings of happiness and well-being.

One reason for these benefits is that nature has a way of slowing us down and grounding us in the present moment. When we're surrounded by the beauty of the natural world, we're reminded of the bigger picture of life. We're reminded that there's more to the world than our daily tasks and to-do lists. We're reminded that we're part of something larger and more complex than ourselves.

Another reason for the healing power of nature is that it encourages us to move our bodies and get active. Whether we're hiking, swimming, or just taking a leisurely walk, being outdoors often involves physical activity. This can be especially beneficial for those of us who spend most of our days sitting at desks. Moving our bodies can help us release tension, improve our circulation, and boost our energy levels.

Perhaps one of the most important benefits of spending time in nature is that it can help us develop a deeper sense of gratitude and appreciation for the world around us. When we take the time to notice the beauty of a sunset, the sound of a babbling brook, or the feel of a gentle breeze on our skin, we're reminded of the wonder and magic of the world. We're reminded that there's so much to be grateful for, even in the midst of difficult times.

So how can we incorporate more nature into our lives? There are many ways to do so, even if we live in urban areas or have busy schedules. Here are a few ideas:

1. Take a walk in a local park or nature reserve

2. Go for a bike ride along a scenic trail
3. Spend a day at the beach or lake
4. Plant a garden or tend to indoor plants
5. Take a camping or hiking trip
6. Practice yoga or meditation outdoors
7. Take up a nature-based hobby, such as bird-watching or photography

Of course, it's important to remember that spending time in nature is not a cure-all for all of our problems. We may still face challenges and difficulties, even when we're surrounded by the beauty of the natural world. But by incorporating more nature into our lives, we can cultivate a deeper sense of peace, gratitude, and connection. We can remind ourselves of the beauty and wonder of the world, and find solace and comfort in the healing power of the outdoors.

In addition to these personal benefits, there are also larger societal benefits to spending time in nature. For example, studies have shown that access to green spaces can improve community health, reduce crime rates, and enhance social cohesion. By investing in parks, green spaces, and other outdoor areas, we can create healthier, happier, and more resilient communities.

- Nature can help us reduce stress:

One of the most common benefits of spending time in nature is the ability to reduce stress. Being in natural environments has been shown to lower cortisol levels, a hormone associated with stress. Additionally, spending time in nature can help us shift our focus away from our worries and concerns and onto the present moment. This can help us feel more calm and centered, even in the midst of stressful situations.

- Nature can improve our mood:

Being in natural environments has been shown to increase our feelings of happiness and well-being. This may be due to the fact that nature offers a respite from the overstimulation of modern life. In nature, we can slow down and take in our surroundings, which can have a calming and mood-boosting effect.

- Nature can improve our cognitive function:

Research has shown that spending time in nature can improve our cognitive function, including our ability to focus and pay attention, because nature offers a restorative environment that can help us recharge our mental batteries.

- Nature can provide us with a sense of awe and wonder:

Spending time in nature can help us tap into our sense of awe and wonder. When we're surrounded by the beauty of the natural world, we're reminded of the vastness and complexity of the universe. This can help us feel more connected to something larger than ourselves, which can be both humbling and inspiring.

- Nature can improve our physical health:

In addition to the mental health benefits of spending time in nature, there are also physical health benefits. For example, being in natural environments has been shown to lower blood pressure, improve cardiovascular health, and boost our immune systems.

These are just a few examples of the many ways in which nature can heal and benefit us. Whether we're seeking stress relief, mental clarity, or a deeper sense of connection, spending time in nature can help us achieve these goals. By incorporating more nature into our lives, we can add a sense of peace, gratitude, and connection that can benefit us both personally and as a society.

In conclusion, nature has the power to heal us in profound ways. Whether we're seeking stress relief, mental clarity, or simply a deeper connection to the world around us, spending time in nature can help us achieve these goals. By incorporating more nature into our lives, we can cultivate a sense of peace, gratitude, and connection that can benefit us both personally and as a society. So the next time you're feeling overwhelmed or disconnected, try stepping outside and taking a deep breath of fresh air. You may be surprised at how much nature has to offer.

CHAPTER SEVEN

Simplicity: The Beauty in Minimalism

The concept of minimalism has been around for centuries, but it has recently gained a lot of attention. Minimalism is all about simplifying your life and focusing on what really matters. It's about reducing clutter, both physical and mental, and eliminating anything that doesn't add value to your life. In this chapter, we will explore how simplicity and minimalism can bring beauty to our lives.

let's define minimalism, minimalism is the intentional decision to live with less. This can mean different things to different people, but it generally involves simplifying your possessions, your schedule, your relationships, and your mindset. Minimalism is about focusing on what truly matters to you and letting go of anything that doesn't align with those priorities.

Minimalism is often associated with aesthetic beauty, but it is more than just a visual style. It's a mindset, a way of life. When we embrace minimalism, we begin to appreciate the beauty in simplicity. We learn to appreciate the things that matter most in our lives, and we let go of the things that are holding us back.

One of the biggest benefits of minimalism is the freedom it provides. When we simplify our lives, we reduce our dependence on material possessions, and we become more self-sufficient. We learn to live with less and find joy in the simple things. We become less focused on accumulating things and more focused on experiences, relationships, and personal growth. When we live with less, we can be more flexible and adaptable. We aren't tied down by material possessions or a rigid schedule. This freedom can lead to greater creativity and innovation, as we have more mental and physical space to explore new ideas and experiences.

Minimalism can also help us become more productive. When we have fewer distractions, we can focus on our goals and priorities. We can eliminate the mental clutter that prevents us from making progress, and we can create a clear path forward. We become more intentional with our time and energy, and we can achieve more with less.

Simplicity can also help us find peace and happiness. When we are surrounded by clutter, it can be difficult to relax and find calm. But when we simplify our environment, we create a sense of order and tranquility. We can breathe easier, and we can find joy in the little things. We learn to appreciate the beauty in our surroundings, and we become more grateful for what we have.

Minimalism can also have a positive impact on our relationships. When we focus on the people in our lives, rather than material possessions, we build stronger connections. We learn to appreciate the value of quality time with loved ones, and we create deeper bonds. We also learn to communicate more effectively, and we can resolve conflicts more easily.

Another benefit of minimalism is that it can have a positive impact on the environment. When we consume less, we reduce our carbon footprint and help protect the planet. We also become more aware of the impact our actions have on the world around us, and we can make more conscious choices.

simplicity and minimalism can bring beauty to our lives. They can help us find freedom, productivity, peace, happiness, and stronger relationships. By letting go of the things that don't add value to our lives, we can create space for the things that do. We can learn to appreciate the beauty in the simple things, and we can live a more intentional and fulfilling life.

Minimalism can also help us become more mindful and intentional. When we live with less, we become more aware of the choices we make and the impact those choices have on our lives and the world around us. We become more deliberate in our decision-making, and we can focus on the things that truly matter to us.

Another benefit of minimalism is the reduction in stress and overwhelm. When we simplify our lives, we reduce the mental clutter that can lead to anxiety and burnout. We can create more time and space for self-care, relaxation, and rejuvenation. We can also reduce the physical clutter in our homes and workspaces, which can lead to greater efficiency and productivity.

Minimalism can also help us become more environmentally conscious. When we live with less, we consume fewer resources and produce less waste. We can make more sustainable choices and reduce our impact on the planet. Additionally, by reducing our reliance on material possessions, we can shift our focus towards experiences and relationships, which can have a positive impact on our personal and professional lives.

Finally, minimalism can bring a sense of peace and contentment to our lives. When we let go of the things that don't serve us, we create space for the things that bring us joy and fulfillment. We can find beauty in the simple things and appreciate the present moment. We can also build stronger connections with the people in our lives and cultivate a greater sense of community and belonging.

In summary, minimalism is a powerful tool for simplifying our lives and finding greater meaning and purpose. By focusing on what truly matters to us, we can create more freedom, mindfulness, and contentment. Whether it's simplifying our possessions, our schedules, our relationships, or our mindset, minimalism can help us live a more intentional and fulfilling life.

CHAPTER EIGHT

Laughter: The Benefits of Humour

Laughter is a universal language that transcends culture, age, and language barriers. It is a powerful tool that can connect people, relieve stress, and promote a sense of well-being.

In this chapter, we will explore the benefits of humour and laughter and how it can positively impact our personal and professional lives.

Physical Benefits of Laughter

Laughter has been linked to numerous physical benefits, including reducing stress, improving the immune system, and decreasing pain. When we laugh, our bodies release endorphins, which are natural painkillers that help us feel good. Endorphins also reduce the levels of stress hormones in the body, such as cortisol and adrenaline, which can lead to decreased blood pressure and improved heart health.

Laughter also promotes the production of antibodies, which help fight infections and diseases. This means that laughter can boost our immune system, helping us stay healthy and recover faster from illnesses.

Psychological Benefits of Laughter

In addition to physical benefits, laughter also has numerous psychological benefits. It has been shown to reduce anxiety, depression, and improve overall mood. When we laugh, our brain releases dopamine, a neurotransmitter associated with pleasure and reward. This can help us feel happier and more relaxed.

Laughter can also improve our cognitive function, such as memory and creativity. When we are in a relaxed and positive state, our brains are more receptive to new information and creative ideas. This means that incorporating humour into our daily lives can help us become more productive and innovative.

Social Benefits of Laughter

Laughter is a powerful social tool that can help us connect with others and build stronger relationships. When we share a laugh with someone, it creates a sense of bonding and trust. Humour can also diffuse tense situations and help us communicate more effectively.

In a professional setting, incorporating humour into presentations or meetings can help engage and connect with colleagues and clients. It can also help break down barriers and create a more relaxed and productive atmosphere.

How to Incorporate Humour into Your Life

Incorporating humour into our daily lives doesn't have to be complicated. Here are some simple ways to add more laughter and joy into your life:

- Watch a funny movie or TV show:

Laughter is contagious, and watching a funny movie or TV show can help you relax and unwind.

- Spend time with friends who make you laugh:

Surrounding yourself with people who have a good sense of humour can help improve your mood and create positive memories.

- Attend a comedy show or open mic night:

Live comedy can be a fun and exciting way to experience laughter and connect with others.

- Read a funny book or comic:

Reading something funny can be a great way to escape from stress and immerse yourself in a lighthearted world.

- Incorporate humour into your work:

Adding a little humour to presentations or meetings can help engage and connect with colleagues and clients.

Laughter is a powerful tool that can improve our physical, psychological, and social well-being. By incorporating humour into our daily lives, we can reduce stress, boost our immune system, and improve our overall mood. So take some time to laugh and enjoy the simple things in life. It might just be the key to your happiness and success.

Laughter and humour have numerous benefits beyond what was discussed

- laughter can improve our emotional intelligence.

Emotional intelligence is the ability to recognize, understand, and manage our own emotions, as well as the emotions of others. When we laugh, we are often able to see situations from a different perspective, which can help us gain a better understanding of others and their emotions.

- laughter can be a powerful stress management tool.

When we are stressed, our bodies release cortisol, which can lead to numerous negative health effects, such as high blood pressure and increased risk of heart disease. However, when we laugh, our bodies release endorphins, which can help counteract the negative effects of cortisol and reduce stress levels.

- laughter can improve our relationships.

When we share a laugh with someone, it creates a sense of intimacy and trust. This can be especially important in romantic relationships, where shared laughter can help couples bond and connect on a deeper level.

- laughter can improve our problem-solving abilities.

When we are in a positive and relaxed state, we are often more open to new ideas and creative solutions. By incorporating humour into our daily lives, we can help cultivate this positive state and improve our ability to solve problems.

- laughter can be a powerful tool for coping with difficult situations.

When we face challenging times, it can be easy to become overwhelmed and stressed. However, by finding humour in even the toughest situations, we can help reduce stress levels and gain a sense of control over our emotions.

In conclusion, laughter and humour have numerous benefits beyond what was discussed in the previous chapter. By incorporating humour into our daily lives, we can improve our emotional intelligence, manage stress, strengthen our relationships, enhance problem-solving abilities, and cope with difficult situations. So don't be afraid to laugh and find the humour in life's ups and downs. It might just be the key to a happier and more successful life.

CHAPTER NINE

Creativity: The Joy of Making

There is a certain joy that comes with the act of creating. Whether it is drawing, painting, writing, building, or cooking, the act of making something with our own hands brings a sense of satisfaction that cannot be found anywhere else. Creativity is not just a form of self-expression; it is a way of life that can bring joy, fulfillment, and success to all aspects of our lives.

Creativity is the ability to come up with new and innovative ideas, and to express them in unique and interesting ways. It is the ability to think outside the box, to look at things from a different perspective, and to come up with solutions to problems that others may not see. Creativity is not limited to the arts; it can be applied to all areas of life, from business and finance to science and technology.

The joy of making something with our own hands is a primal instinct that has been with us since the beginning of human history. From the first cave paintings to the most intricate sculptures and paintings of today, the act of creating has always been a part of our human experience. It is a way of connecting with our inner selves, of expressing our emotions and feelings, and of leaving our mark on the world.

There are many benefits to embracing creativity in our lives. For one, it can be a great stress reliever. The act of creating something can be incredibly therapeutic, allowing us to focus our minds and relax our bodies. It can also help us to develop new skills and abilities, as we learn to think in new and different ways.

Creativity can also lead to greater success in our personal and professional lives. In business, those who are able to come up with innovative ideas and solutions are often the ones who rise to the top. In our personal lives, creativity can help us to express ourselves more effectively, to connect with others, and to find joy and meaning in the world around us.

There are many different forms of creativity, and each person may find joy in different ways. Some may find it in painting or drawing, while others may find it in writing or music. Still others may find it in cooking or gardening. Whatever form it takes, the act of creating something with our own hands can bring a sense of satisfaction and fulfillment that cannot be found anywhere else.

To embrace creativity in our lives, we must first be willing to take risks and try new things. We must be willing to fail, to make mistakes, and to learn from them. We must be willing to step outside our comfort zones and challenge ourselves to think in new and different ways.

We must also be willing to make time for creativity in our lives. In today's fast-paced world, it can be easy to get caught up in the daily grind and forget about the things that truly bring us joy. But by setting aside time each day or each week to pursue our creative passions, we can cultivate a sense of purpose and meaning in our lives that can lead to greater happiness and success.

There have been several scientific studies on the benefits of creativity in our lives, which help to explain why the act of creating can bring us so much joy and fulfillment.

One study, published in the Journal of Positive Psychology in 2016, found that engaging in creative activities can lead to greater well-being and positive emotions. The study asked participants to engage in a creative activity for just 45 minutes a day for a week, and found that those who did so reported feeling more relaxed, energized, and happy than those who did not engage in creative activities.

Another study, published in the Journal of Creative Behavior in 2013, found that creativity can help to reduce stress levels and improve mood. The study asked participants to engage in a creative task while their stress levels were monitored, and found that those who engaged in the creative task showed a significant decrease in stress levels compared to those who did not engage in the task.

There have also been studies on the benefits of creativity in the workplace. One study, published in the Journal of Business and Psychology in 2015, found that employees who were encouraged to engage in creative activities at work reported greater job satisfaction and a higher sense of well-being than those who were not encouraged to do so.

Finally, there have been studies on the link between creativity and success in life. One study, published in the Journal of Creative Behavior in 2018, found that individuals who engaged in creative activities were more likely to be successful in their careers and personal lives than those who did not. The study found that creativity can lead to greater problem-solving abilities, greater flexibility in thinking, and greater ability to adapt to changing circumstances, all of which are important qualities for success in life.

Overall, the scientific research supports the idea that creativity can bring us joy, fulfillment, and success in all aspects of our lives. Whether we are engaging in creative activities for personal pleasure or for professional development, the act of creating can have a powerful positive impact on our well-being and our ability to succeed in life.

In conclusion, creativity is a vital part of the human experience, and the joy of making something with our own hands is a primal instinct that has been with us since the beginning of time. By embracing creativity in our lives, we can find joy, fulfillment, and success in all aspects of our lives. So take a risk, try something new, and see where your creativity can take you. You may be surprised at the joy and fulfillment you find along the way.

CHAPTER TEN

Learning: The Power of Curiosity

The human mind is an ever-curious entity. It seeks answers to questions that might not have any real-world significance. We explore new horizons, discover hidden treasures, and ask the unasked. Our ability to learn and adapt to new information has been instrumental in our progress as a species. We have been able to create wonders from scratch, discover and invent things that would have been impossible without the innate curiosity that drives us. In this chapter, we will delve into the power of curiosity in our learning process.

The Importance of Curiosity

Curiosity is the fuel that drives our learning engine. It is the desire to know more, to discover the unknown, and to solve the unexplained. Without curiosity, we wouldn't have made the progress that we have made so far. It is what makes us ask the questions, seek the answers, and explore new possibilities. In other words, curiosity is the key to unlocking our full potential.

Curiosity plays a crucial role in every aspect of our lives, from our personal relationships to our professional careers. It helps us understand the world around us and gives us a sense of purpose. Curiosity motivates us to learn new skills, gain knowledge, and become better versions of ourselves. It enables us to see things from a different perspective and to find innovative solutions to problems that seem unsolvable.

The Power of Asking Questions

Questions are the tools that we use to explore the unknown. They help us gain clarity, understand complex concepts, and find new ways of doing things. The more questions we ask, the more we learn. Asking questions not only helps us gain knowledge, but it also helps us develop critical thinking skills. It allows us to evaluate ideas, challenge assumptions, and seek evidence to support our claims.

Asking questions also helps us connect with others. It shows that we are interested in what they have to say and that we value their opinion. It opens up lines of communication and helps us build relationships. In a professional setting, asking questions is a valuable skill that can help us identify problems and find solutions. It helps us stay informed about our industry and enables us to make informed decisions.

The Role of Curiosity in Learning

Curiosity and learning go hand in hand. It is impossible to learn anything without being curious about it. When we are curious about a subject, we are motivated to learn more about it. We seek out information, read books, watch videos, and talk to experts. Our curiosity drives us to become experts ourselves.

Curiosity also helps us overcome obstacles in the learning process. When we encounter a difficult problem or concept, our curiosity motivates us to keep going. It makes us want to understand the problem and find a solution. It helps us persist through the challenges and come out on the other side with a deeper understanding of the subject.

Curiosity also helps us develop a growth mindset. When we are curious, we are open to new experiences and ideas. We are willing to take risks and try new things. This mindset is essential for learning because it enables us to embrace challenges and learn from our mistakes. It helps us see failure as an opportunity for growth, rather than a setback.

How to Cultivate Curiosity

Curiosity is not something that we are born with; it is a skill that we can learn. Here are a few ways to cultivate curiosity in your life:

- Ask questions:

As we discussed earlier, asking questions is the key to learning. Make it a habit to ask questions about everything that interests you.

- Follow your interests:

Pursue activities that interest you, whether it's reading, watching documentaries, or attending workshops. The more you engage in activities that interest you, the more you will learn.

- Be open-minded:

Be willing to consider ideas that are different from your own. This will help you see things from different perspectives and expand your knowledge.

- Take risks:

Trying new things can be scary, but it can also be incredibly rewarding. Be willing to step outside of your comfort zone and try something new.

- Embrace failure:

Failure is a natural part of the learning process. Instead of seeing failure as a setback, embrace it as an opportunity to learn and grow.

- Keep learning:

Learning is a lifelong process. Make it a habit to learn something new every day. This could be as simple as reading a book or watching a TED Talk.

There have been several scientific studies that have explored the relationship between curiosity and learning. In one study published in the journal Neuron in 2014, researchers found that curiosity enhances learning and memory. Participants who were more curious about a topic were more likely to remember the information they learned about it.

Another study published in the journal Psychological Science in 2015 found that curiosity can enhance the learning of new information, particularly when that information is not directly related to a person's goals. The study found that people who were more curious about a topic were more likely to remember information that was not directly relevant to their goals, but was still related to the topic they were interested in.

A study published in the journal Personality and Social Psychology Bulletin in 2018 found that curiosity is associated with greater academic achievement. The study found that students who were more curious about a topic were more likely to engage in deep learning, which is associated with greater academic achievement.

Additionally, a study published in the journal Neuron in 2016 found that curiosity can enhance learning by increasing activity in the brain's reward system. The study found that when people were more curious about a topic, they were more likely to remember information related to that topic and had increased activity in the brain's reward system, which is associated with learning and memory.

Overall, these studies suggest that curiosity plays an important role in the learning process. It motivates us to explore new topics, ask questions, and seek out information. By enhancing learning and memory, curiosity can help us achieve greater academic and professional success.

In Conclusion, Curiosity is a powerful force that drives our learning process. It motivates us to explore new horizons, seek answers to questions, and discover new possibilities. Without curiosity, we wouldn't have made the progress that we have made so far. Cultivating curiosity is essential for personal and professional growth. By asking questions, following our interests, being open-minded, taking risks, embracing failure, and keeping learning, we can unlock the full potential of our curiosity and continue to learn and grow throughout our lives. So, embrace your curiosity, and let it lead you to new and exciting discoveries!

CHAPTER ELEVEN

Silence: The Importance of Stillness

In a world that is always on the go, it can be easy to forget the importance of stillness and silence. Yet, these two things are essential for our mental and emotional well-being, and they can have a profound impact on our personal and professional lives. In this chapter, we'll explore the importance of silence and stillness, how to cultivate them, and how they can help us find happiness and success in life.

What is Silence?

Silence is the absence of sound, but it's much more than that. It's a state of being, a space where we can quiet our minds and connect with ourselves on a deeper level. It's a place of peace and tranquility, where we can reflect on our lives and find the answers we need.

Why is Silence Important?

Silence is important for many reasons, but perhaps the most significant is that it allows us to connect with our true selves. When we're surrounded by noise and distractions, it can be challenging to listen to our inner voice and connect with our intuition. However, when we're in a state of silence, we can tune out the noise and focus on what's truly important.

Silence can also help us reduce stress and anxiety. When we're constantly bombarded by noise and stimuli, it can be overwhelming for our minds and bodies. However, when we take the time to be still and quiet, we can give our minds and bodies a much-needed break, reducing our stress levels and promoting relaxation.

How to Cultivate Silence

Cultivating silence can be challenging in a world that is always on the go, but it's not impossible. Here are a few tips to help you find moments of stillness and silence in your daily life:

- Create a quiet space:

Designate a space in your home or office that is free from distractions and noise. Make this space your sanctuary, where you can go to be alone with your thoughts and find peace.

- Take a walk in nature:

Nature is one of the best places to find stillness and silence. Take a walk in the park, hike in the woods, or simply sit by a river or lake and enjoy the peace and tranquility.

- Practice meditation:

Meditation is a powerful tool for cultivating silence and stillness. Find a quiet place to sit, close your eyes, and focus on your breath. As thoughts arise, simply observe them without judgment and let them go.

- Turn off your devices:

In today's world, we're constantly connected to our devices. However, turning them off for a set period each day can help us disconnect from the noise and distractions and connect with ourselves.

How Silence Can Help You Find Success and Happiness

Silence and stillness can help us find success and happiness in many ways. Here are just a few:

- Increased self-awareness:

When we're in a state of silence and stillness, we can connect with our inner selves and become more aware of our thoughts, feelings, and desires. This self-awareness can help us make better decisions, set clearer goals, and live a more fulfilling life.

- Better focus:

When we're surrounded by noise and distractions, it can be challenging to focus on the task at hand. However, when we cultivate stillness and silence, we can train our minds to focus more effectively, increasing our productivity and success.

- Improved relationships:

Silence can also help us improve our relationships with others. When we take the time to listen to others without judgment, we can deepen our understanding and compassion, leading to stronger and more fulfilling relationships.

- Greater peace and contentment:

Silence and stillness can bring us greater peace and contentment in life. When we're constantly on the go, we can easily become stressed and overwhelmed, but when we take the time to be still and quiet, we can find a sense of calm and balance that can help us navigate life's challenges with greater ease and grace.

There has been a significant amount of research conducted on the benefits of silence and stillness for our mental and emotional well-being. Here are a few examples of research studies that demonstrate the importance of cultivating silence and stillness in our lives:

- Improved Cognitive Functioning:

A study published in the journal Frontiers in Human Neuroscience in 2013 found that just two minutes of silence can help improve cognitive function and creativity.

The study found that when participants were exposed to silence, they showed increased activity in the brain's default mode network, which is associated with introspection and self-awareness.

- Reduced Stress and Anxiety:

A study published in the journal Heart in 2006 found that just two minutes of silence can help reduce stress and lower blood pressure. The study found that when participants were exposed to two minutes of silence, their blood pressure dropped, and their heart rate slowed down, indicating a reduction in stress levels.

- Increased Focus and Productivity:

A study published in the journal Applied Cognitive Psychology in 2010 found that short periods of silence can help improve focus and productivity. The study found that participants who were exposed to silence for just two minutes showed improved cognitive performance and were better able to focus on their tasks.

- Improved Relationships:

A study published in the journal Communication Research in 2011 found that silence can help improve communication and relationships between individuals. The study found that when couples engaged in moments of silence during their conversations, they showed increased empathy and understanding towards each other.

- Improved Mental Health:

A study published in the journal Psychiatry Research in 2015 found that mindfulness-based meditation, which involves cultivating stillness and silence, can help improve symptoms of anxiety and depression. The study found that participants who practiced mindfulness-based meditation showed reduced symptoms of anxiety and depression and increased feelings of well-being.

research studies have shown that cultivating stillness and silence can have significant benefits for our mental and emotional well-being, including improved cognitive functioning, reduced stress and anxiety, increased focus and productivity, improved relationships, and improved mental health. So, it's essential to take the time to be still and silent in our daily lives, even if it's just for a few minutes each day, to reap these benefits and live a happier, healthier life.

In Conclusion, Silence and stillness may seem like small things, but they have the power to transform our lives in profound ways. By cultivating these qualities, we can connect with our true selves, reduce stress and anxiety, improve our focus and productivity, deepen our relationships with others, and find greater peace and contentment in life. So, take some time today to be still and silent, and see how it can change your life for the better.

CHAPTER TWELVE

Empathy: Understanding Others

Empathy is the ability to understand and share the feelings of others. It is a vital component of emotional intelligence, and it is what allows us to connect with others on a deep and meaningful level. In today's fast-paced world, where we are constantly bombarded with information, it is easy to become disconnected from those around us. But with empathy, we can learn to understand and appreciate others, and in doing so, enrich our own lives.

What is Empathy?

Empathy is often confused with sympathy, but the two are very different. Sympathy is feeling sorry for someone else's situation, while empathy is the ability to put yourself in someone else's shoes and experience their emotions. Empathy requires us to be fully present and engaged with the other person, to listen carefully to their words, and to observe their body language.

Empathy is not about agreeing with someone or condoning their behavior. It is about acknowledging their feelings and validating their experience. It is about creating a safe space for them to express themselves without fear of judgment or rejection.

Why is Empathy Important?

Empathy is crucial for building strong relationships, whether personal or professional. When we take the time to understand and connect with others, we build trust and respect. We become better listeners, better problem solvers, and better communicators. Empathy helps us to appreciate diversity, to see things from different perspectives, and to find common ground with those who may seem different from us.

In the workplace, empathy is becoming increasingly important as teams become more diverse and global. It is essential for effective collaboration, conflict resolution, and leadership. Empathy helps leaders to understand their team members' strengths and weaknesses, to provide support and guidance, and to create a positive work environment.

How to practice Empathy

Empathy is not something that comes naturally to everyone. Some people may be more naturally empathetic than others, but everyone can learn to be more empathetic with practice. Here are some ideas for developing empathy:

- Listen actively:

When someone is speaking to you, give them your full attention. Put away your phone, make eye contact, and nod and respond to show that you are engaged.

- Practice non-judgment:

Try to put aside your own biases and judgments and focus on the other person's experience. Acknowledge their feelings without criticizing or minimizing them.

- Observe body language:

Pay attention to the other person's body language, as it can often communicate more than words. Notice their facial expressions, gestures, and posture.

- Ask questions:

Don't assume that you know what the other person is thinking or feeling. Ask questions to clarify and understand their perspective.

- Practice perspective-taking:

Try to put yourself in the other person's shoes and imagine how you would feel in their situation. This can help you to better understand and empathize with their experience.

- Show compassion:

Even if you don't fully understand someone's experience, you can still show compassion and support.

Sometimes just being there for someone and listening can make all the difference.

Empathy in Action

Empathy is not just a theoretical concept - it is something that we can put into practice every day. Here are some examples of empathy in action:

- Listening to a friend who is going through a difficult time and offering support and validation.

- Recognizing and acknowledging the feelings of a team member who is struggling with a project and offering assistance or resources to help them succeed.

- Showing understanding and compassion to a customer who is frustrated with a product or service, and working to resolve their issue.

- Taking the time to learn about and appreciate different cultures and perspectives, and seeking out opportunities to connect with people from diverse backgrounds.

Empathy is a fundamental aspect of our human experience, and one that has the power to transform our personal and professional relationships in profound ways. When we practice empathy, we are essentially stepping into another person's shoes and trying to understand their experience from their perspective. This requires us to be fully present and engaged with the other person, to listen carefully to their words, and to observe their body language.

By developing empathy, we are able to build stronger connections with others, as we demonstrate that we value their feelings and experiences. This can help to create a more positive and supportive environment, whether it be in our personal relationships with friends and family, or in our professional relationships with colleagues and clients.

Empathy is an important skill for effective leadership. When leaders are empathetic, they are better able to understand and support their team members, which can lead to increased productivity, better problem-solving, and a more positive work culture. Leaders who lack empathy, on the other hand, may struggle to connect with their team members, and may be perceived as distant or uncaring.

It is important to note that empathy does not mean that we have to agree with everything that someone else says or does. It is simply about acknowledging and validating their feelings and experiences, even if we do not necessarily agree with them. By practicing empathy, we are able to create a safe and supportive space for others to express themselves, which can lead to greater trust and respect in our relationships.

Overall, empathy is a vital aspect of our emotional intelligence, and one that we should all strive to cultivate in our lives. By actively listening, practicing non-judgment, observing body language, asking questions, and showing compassion, we can improve our ability to empathize with others and create a more harmonious and connected world.

Empathy is a powerful tool for building strong relationships, fostering understanding and respect, and creating a positive impact in the world. By developing our ability to empathize with others, we can improve our personal and professional relationships, as well as make a meaningful contribution to society.

In our busy and hectic lives, it can be easy to become focused on our own needs and goals. However, by taking the time to truly understand and connect with others, we can expand our own perspectives and enrich our lives in ways we never thought possible. Empathy is not just about helping others - it is also about helping ourselves to become more compassionate, open-minded, and fulfilled individuals.

In conclusion, empathy is an essential aspect of our human experience, and one that we should all strive to cultivate in our lives. By practicing active listening, non-judgment, perspective-taking, and compassion, we can improve our relationships with others and create a more harmonious and connected world. So let us all take the time to understand and appreciate those around us, and in doing so, discover the beauty and richness of simple things in life.

CHAPTER THIRTEEN

Forgiveness: Letting Go of Grudges

Forgiveness is one of the simplest yet most powerful things in life. It involves letting go of grudges, resentments, and anger towards someone who has wronged you. Forgiveness is not easy, but it is essential to living a happy and successful life. In this chapter, we will explore the importance of forgiveness and how to practice it in our daily lives.

The Power of Forgiveness

Forgiveness is a powerful tool that can transform your life. It can heal emotional wounds, mend broken relationships, and free you from the burden of anger and resentment. When you hold onto grudges, you are carrying a heavy load that can weigh you down, both emotionally and physically. Studies have shown that forgiveness can reduce stress and anxiety, lower blood pressure, and improve overall health and well-being.

Forgiveness can also improve your relationships. When you forgive someone, you open the door for reconciliation and a deeper understanding of one another. Forgiveness can help build trust and strengthen bonds between people. It can also help you let go of toxic relationships that are holding you back.

The Benefits of Forgiveness

- Increased happiness:

Forgiveness can lead to greater happiness and life satisfaction. Letting go of anger and resentment can help you focus on the positive things in life and cultivate gratitude.

- Improved health:

Forgiveness can reduce stress, anxiety, and depression, leading to improved physical and mental health. It can also lower blood pressure and boost the immune system.

- Stronger relationships:

Forgiveness can improve relationships and build trust. It can also help you let go of toxic relationships that are holding you back.

- Personal growth:

Forgiveness can help you grow and develop as a person. It can teach you empathy, compassion, and understanding.

How to Practice Forgiveness

Practicing forgiveness is not easy, but it is essential to living a happy and successful life. Here are some ways to help you practice forgiveness:

- Acknowledge your feelings:

Before you can forgive someone, you need to acknowledge your feelings. Take the time to reflect on how the person's actions made you feel and the impact it had on your life.

- Choose to forgive:

Forgiveness is a choice. You need to decide that you are willing to let go of your anger and resentment and forgive the person who wronged you.

- Let go of grudges:

Holding onto grudges only hurts you. Let go of your anger and resentment towards the person who wronged you.

- Practice empathy:

Try to understand the other person's perspective and why they did what they did. This can help you develop empathy and compassion towards them.

- Communicate:

If possible, communicate with the person who wronged you. Let them know how their actions affected you and that you are choosing to forgive them.

- Seek support:

Forgiveness is not always easy, and it can be helpful to seek support from a therapist or counselor. They can help you work through your feelings and develop strategies for forgiveness.

Forgiveness is a complex and nuanced concept, and there are many different aspects to it that can be explored in greater detail.

One of the most important aspects of forgiveness is the idea of letting go. When we hold onto anger and resentment towards someone who has wronged us, we are essentially holding onto a burden that can weigh us down and prevent us from moving forward. Letting go of that burden can be incredibly liberating and empowering, and it can help us to feel lighter and more free.

Another important aspect of forgiveness is empathy. When we forgive someone, we are essentially choosing to try to understand their perspective and see things from their point of view. This can be difficult, especially if the person's actions have caused us a great deal of pain or hurt. However, it can also be incredibly healing and can help us to develop greater compassion and understanding towards others.

Forgiveness can also be an important tool for personal growth and development. When we forgive someone, we are essentially choosing to take the high road and rise above our own hurt and pain. This can be a difficult thing to do, but it can also be incredibly empowering and can help us to develop greater resilience and strength.

It's important to note that forgiveness does not necessarily mean forgetting or condoning the actions of the person who wronged us. It is possible to forgive someone while still recognizing that what they did was wrong or hurtful. However, forgiveness does involve choosing to let go of our anger and resentment towards that person, and choosing to move forward in a more positive and productive way.

In order to practice forgiveness, it can be helpful to cultivate a sense of mindfulness and self-awareness. By paying attention to our own thoughts and feelings, we can become more aware of when we are holding onto grudges or anger towards someone else. We can also begin to develop greater empathy and compassion towards others by actively trying to put ourselves in their shoes and understand their perspective.

Overall, forgiveness is an incredibly powerful tool that can have far-reaching benefits in our personal and professional lives. By practicing forgiveness, we can improve our relationships, cultivate greater happiness and well-being, and become more resilient and compassionate individuals.

Forgiveness is one of the simplest yet most powerful things in life. It involves letting go of grudges, resentments, and anger towards someone who has wronged you. Forgiveness is not easy, but it is essential to living a happy and successful life. When you forgive someone, you open the door for reconciliation and a deeper understanding of one another. Forgiveness can help build trust and strengthen bonds between people. It can also help you let go of toxic relationships that are holding you back. By practicing forgiveness, you can improve your health, increase happiness, and grow as a person.

CHAPTER FOURTEEN

Health - Taking Care of Our Bodies

In our quest for happiness and success, we often overlook one of the most important factors: our health. Our bodies are our greatest asset and taking care of them is vital for achieving our goals and living a fulfilling life. In this chapter, we will explore the various ways in which we can take care of our bodies and maintain good health.

Exercise

Regular exercise is crucial for maintaining a healthy body. It not only helps us to maintain a healthy weight but also keeps our heart, lungs, and muscles strong. Exercise also releases endorphins, which are natural mood-boosters that can reduce stress and anxiety. It's important to find an exercise routine that suits your lifestyle and preferences. Whether it's jogging, yoga, or weightlifting, find an activity that you enjoy and try to incorporate it into your daily routine.

Regular exercise has been shown to have numerous health benefits, including reducing the risk of chronic diseases such as obesity, diabetes, and heart disease. A

2015 study published in the Lancet found that physical inactivity is responsible for 5.3 million deaths worldwide each year. In addition to reducing the risk of chronic diseases, exercise has also been shown to have a positive impact on mental health. A 2018 study published in The Lancet Psychiatry found that people who exercise have 43% fewer days of poor mental health than those who do not exercise.

Eat a Balanced Diet

Eating a balanced diet is essential for maintaining good health. A diet that is rich in fruits, vegetables, whole grains, and lean proteins provides our bodies with the nutrients they need to function properly. It's also important to avoid processed and high-sugar foods, as these can lead to health problems such as obesity, diabetes, and heart disease.

Eating a balanced diet has also been shown to have numerous health benefits. A 2017 study published in the Journal of the American College of Cardiology found that a diet that is high in fruits, vegetables, whole grains, nuts, and seeds is associated with a lower risk of heart disease. In addition, a 2019 study published in JAMA Internal Medicine found that a plant-based diet can reduce the risk of developing type 2 diabetes. On the other hand, a diet that is high in processed foods and sugar has been linked to a range of health problems, including obesity, diabetes, and heart disease.

Get Enough Sleep

Getting enough sleep is essential for our physical and mental health. A lack of sleep can lead to a range of health problems, including fatigue, irritability, and difficulty concentrating. Adults should aim to get between seven and nine hours of sleep per night, while children and teenagers need even more. Establishing a regular sleep routine and creating a comfortable sleep environment can help ensure that you get the rest you need.

Getting enough sleep is essential for our physical and mental health. A 2017 study published in the Journal of Sleep Research found that people who get less than six hours of sleep per night are at a higher risk of developing obesity, type 2 diabetes, and heart disease. In addition, a lack of sleep has been shown to have a negative impact on mental health. A 2018 study published in The Lancet Psychiatry found that sleep problems are associated with an increased risk of developing mental health problems such as depression and anxiety.

Practice Good Hygiene

Practicing good hygiene is crucial for preventing the spread of illness and maintaining good health. This includes washing your hands regularly, covering your mouth when you cough or sneeze, and avoiding close contact with people who are sick. It's also important to keep your living spaces clean and tidy, especially in areas where germs are likely to spread.

Practicing good hygiene is important for preventing the spread of illness. A 2018 study published in the American Journal of Infection Control found that hand hygiene is an effective way to prevent the spread of infectious diseases in healthcare settings. In addition, a 2019 study published in the Journal of Hospital Infection found that implementing a comprehensive infection prevention and control program can reduce the risk of healthcare-associated infections.

Manage Stress

Stress is a normal part of life, but when it becomes chronic, it can lead to a range of health problems, including anxiety and depression. Learning how to manage stress is crucial for maintaining good health. This can include practices such as meditation, deep breathing exercises, or engaging in relaxing activities such as yoga or reading.

Stress has been shown to have a negative impact on both physical and mental health. A 2017 study published in the Journal of Occupational Health Psychology found that job stress is associated with an increased risk of developing type 2 diabetes. In addition, a 2019 study published in the Journal of Affective Disorders found that stress is a risk factor for developing depression. However, there are numerous ways to manage stress, including exercise, meditation, and relaxation techniques.

Avoid Harmful Substances

Avoiding harmful substances such as tobacco and excessive alcohol is crucial for maintaining good health. Smoking can lead to a range of health problems, including lung cancer and heart disease, while excessive alcohol consumption can lead to liver damage, high blood pressure, and other health problems. It's important to seek help if you struggle with addiction or substance abuse.

Avoiding harmful substances such as tobacco and excessive alcohol is important for maintaining good health. A 2018 study published in The Lancet found that tobacco use is responsible for 7.1 million deaths worldwide each year. In addition, a 2019 study published in The Lancet Public Health found that alcohol consumption is responsible for 2.8 million deaths worldwide each year.

Get Regular Checkups

Getting regular checkups and screenings is essential for maintaining good health. This includes regular visits to your doctor, as well as screenings for conditions such as cancer, high blood pressure, and diabetes. By catching health problems early, you can take steps to prevent them from becoming more serious.

Getting regular checkups and screenings is important for detecting health problems early. A 2018 study published in the Journal of the American Medical Association found that regular screening for colorectal cancer can reduce the risk of dying from the disease by up to 50%. In addition, a 2017 study published in the Journal of the American College of Cardiology found that regular checkups and lifestyle interventions can reduce the risk of developing heart disease.

In conclusion, there is ample scientific research to support the importance of taking care of our bodies. By exercising regularly taking care of our bodies is essential for living a happy and successful life. By following these tips, we can maintain good physical and mental health and enjoy all that life has to offer. Remember, small and simple things can make a big difference in our lives, and taking care of our bodies is one of the simplest and most important things we can do.

CHAPTER FIFTEEN

Time: Managing Our Most Valuable Resource

Time is a precious and limited resource that we all have. It is the only resource that we can never get back once it is lost, and yet it is one that we often take for granted. Time is a critical factor in our lives, and how we use it can make a significant difference in our happiness and success.

Managing time is a skill that many people struggle with, and it can be challenging to prioritize and balance all the activities in our personal and professional lives. However, by being mindful of how we spend our time, we can make the most of it and lead a more fulfilling life.

Here are some essential principles to consider when managing our time:

- Identify Your Priorities:

It's essential to understand what is most important to you and prioritize accordingly. This can be a challenging task as we often have competing demands for our time. However, taking the time to identify your values and goals can help you prioritize the activities that align with your priorities.

Start by making a list of your top priorities, such as family, career, health, or personal growth. Next, evaluate how you spend your time currently and identify activities that do not align with your priorities. By doing this, you can identify opportunities to eliminate or delegate tasks that are not critical to your goals and focus on activities that matter most.

- Develop a Routine:

Establishing a routine can help you make the most of your time. It can help you to manage your time more effectively by reducing the amount of time and energy spent on making decisions. By creating a consistent routine, you can automate the activities that are essential to you and free up time for other tasks.

Design a daily schedule that works for you, including time for exercise, work, family, and personal activities. Also, consider the time of day when you are most productive and try to schedule your most important tasks during those times.

- Learn to Say No:

Saying "no" can be challenging, especially when we want to please others or fear missing out on opportunities. However, learning to say "no" can be a powerful tool for managing our time and focusing on our priorities.

Before committing to any new activity, ask yourself if it aligns with your values and goals. If it does not, it may be better to decline the invitation or delegate the task to someone else. By doing this, you can avoid overcommitting yourself and free up time for activities that matter most.

- Use Technology to Your Advantage:

Technology can be both a blessing and a curse when it comes to time management. While it can be a significant distraction, there are also many tools available that can help you manage your time more effectively.

Consider using tools such as time-tracking apps, calendar apps, and project management tools to help you stay organized and focused. These tools can help you identify where you are spending your time and streamline your workflow, making you more efficient and productive.

- Take Time to Recharge:

Taking time to recharge is essential to maintaining productivity and managing our time effectively. It may seem counterintuitive, but taking regular breaks and vacations can actually help us get more done in the long run.

Schedule time for relaxation and self-care activities, such as exercise, meditation, or spending time with loved ones. By taking time to recharge, you can reduce stress and fatigue, increase creativity, and be more focused and productive when you return to work.

- Identify and Eliminate Time Wasters:

Identifying and eliminating time wasters can significantly improve our time management skills. Time wasters are activities that consume our time but do not add any value to our lives or contribute to our goals. Some common time wasters include social media, unnecessary meetings, and excessive multitasking.

To identify your time wasters, try tracking how you spend your time for a week or two. Then, evaluate your results and identify activities that do not align with your priorities or add value to your life. By eliminating time wasters, you can free up more time for activities that matter most.

- Use Time Blocking:

Time blocking is a technique that involves scheduling specific blocks of time for specific tasks. It can help you stay focused and avoid distractions by dedicating specific time slots to particular activities. For instance, you can block off time in your calendar for writing, responding to emails, or attending meetings.

To use time blocking, start by identifying your top priorities and scheduling blocks of time for these activities in your calendar. Make sure to allow for breaks and downtime between tasks to avoid burnout and increase productivity.

- Learn to Delegate:

Delegating tasks to others can help you save time and increase productivity. It involves assigning tasks to someone else who has the necessary skills and expertise to complete the task. Delegating can also help you focus on your core competencies and achieve your goals more efficiently.

To delegate effectively, start by identifying tasks that you can delegate to others. Then, identify individuals or teams who have the necessary skills and experience to complete the task. Finally, communicate your expectations clearly and provide support and guidance as needed.

- Practice Mindfulness:

Mindfulness is a state of being present and fully engaged in the moment. It can help you manage your time more effectively by reducing distractions, increasing focus, and reducing stress. Mindfulness techniques such as meditation, deep breathing, or yoga can help you stay present and focused throughout the day.

To practice mindfulness, start by setting aside time each day for meditation or deep breathing exercises. Focus on your breath and let go of any distracting thoughts or worries. With regular practice, you can develop the habit of mindfulness and improve your time management skills.

In conclusion, managing time effectively is essential to achieving our goals and living a fulfilling life. By identifying our priorities, eliminating time wasters, using time blocking, delegating tasks, and practicing mindfulness, we can make the most of our time and achieve success in both our personal and professional lives. Remember, time is our most valuable resource, and we must use it wisely to achieve our goals and live a meaningful life, time is a precious resource that we must manage wisely to live a fulfilling life. By identifying our priorities, developing a routine, learning to say no, using technology to our advantage, and taking time to recharge, we can make the most of our time and achieve our goals. Remember, time is the one thing we can never get back,

CHAPTER SIXTEEN

Self-Care: Prioritizing Our Own Needs

In today's fast-paced world, people are constantly busy with work, school, and various other responsibilities. With so much going on, it can be easy to forget about taking care of ourselves. However, self-care is crucial for our physical, mental, and emotional well-being. By prioritizing our own needs, we can lead happier and more successful lives.

What is Self-Care?

Self-care refers to any activity or practice that helps us maintain and improve our physical, mental, and emotional health. It is an ongoing process that involves making conscious choices to prioritize our well-being.

Self-care can take many forms, including exercise, meditation, journaling, spending time with loved ones, getting enough sleep, and eating a healthy diet. It is important to note that self-care is not a one-size-fits-all solution. What works for one person may not work for another. Therefore, it is essential to experiment and find what works best for you.

Why is Self-Care Important?

Self-care is essential for several reasons. First and foremost, it helps us maintain our physical health. When we take care of our bodies by eating well, exercising regularly, and getting enough sleep, we reduce the risk of developing various illnesses and diseases.

Self-care is also essential for our mental health. Taking time for ourselves can help reduce stress and anxiety, improve our mood, and boost our self-esteem. When we prioritize our mental health, we become better equipped to handle life's challenges.

Self-care is crucial for our emotional well-being. When we engage in activities that bring us joy and fulfillment, we cultivate a sense of purpose and meaning in our lives. This can lead to greater happiness and overall life satisfaction.

The Importance of Prioritizing Our Own Needs

Many of us are guilty of putting others' needs before our own. We may feel guilty or selfish for taking time for ourselves. However, prioritizing our own needs is essential for our well-being. When we neglect our own needs, we may become burned out, stressed, and unhappy.

Prioritizing our own needs does not mean neglecting the needs of others. Rather, it means taking care of ourselves so that we can better care for others. When we prioritize our own well-being, we become better equipped to handle the demands of our jobs, relationships, and other responsibilities.

Ideas for Prioritizing Self-Care

Prioritizing self-care can be challenging, especially when we are busy with work and other responsibilities. However, there are several strategies we can use to make self-care a priority in our lives:

- Make Time for Self-Care:

One of the most important things we can do is make time for self-care. This may mean carving out time in our schedules for activities that bring us joy, such as reading a book, taking a bath, or going for a walk.

- Set Boundaries:

Setting boundaries is essential for prioritizing self-care. We may need to say no to certain activities or commitments that do not align with our values or priorities.

- Practice Mindfulness:

Practicing mindfulness can help us stay present and focused on the moment. By staying mindful, we can better appreciate the small things in life and cultivate a sense of gratitude.

- Seek Support:

It is essential to seek support from loved ones, friends, or a mental health professional when we need it. By seeking support, we can better cope with life's challenges and maintain our well-being.

- Practice Self-Compassion:

Finally, it is essential to practice self-compassion. We may make mistakes or experience setbacks along the way, but it is important to treat ourselves with kindness and understanding.

Self-care is crucial for our physical, mental, and emotional well-being. By prioritizing our own needs, we can lead happier and more successful lives. It is important to remember that self-care is not selfish or indulgent, but rather a necessary part of maintaining our health and well-being.

We may face obstacles and challenges when trying to prioritize self-care, but there are strategies we can use to make it a priority in our lives. By making time for self-care, setting boundaries, practicing mindfulness, seeking support, and practicing self-compassion, we can prioritize our own needs and lead more fulfilling lives.

In the end, simple things in life often bring us the most joy and fulfillment. By prioritizing self-care, we can develop a sense of purpose and meaning in our lives and lead happier, healthier, and more successful lives.

importance of self-care and how it can benefit us in different aspects of our lives.

Self-care is crucial for our physical health. Our bodies require rest, nutrition, and exercise to function at their best. When we prioritize our own needs and take care of our bodies, we reduce the risk of developing various illnesses and diseases. This, in turn, can lead to increased productivity and energy levels, allowing us to better perform our daily tasks.

Moreover, self-care is essential for our mental health. In today's fast-paced world, stress and anxiety are prevalent, and it can be easy to become overwhelmed. When we engage in self-care practices such as meditation, yoga, or journaling, we can reduce stress and anxiety, improve our mood, and boost our self-esteem. This can improve our relationships with others and enhance our overall quality of life.

Furthermore, self-care is crucial for our emotional well-being. Engaging in activities that bring us joy and fulfillment, such as spending time with loved ones, pursuing hobbies, or volunteering, can help us cultivate a sense of purpose and meaning in our lives. This can lead to greater happiness and overall life satisfaction.

In addition to these benefits, prioritizing our own needs can also help us become better equipped to handle the demands of our daily lives. By taking care of ourselves first, we can better care for others, whether it be our family, friends, or colleagues. We may also find that we have more energy, creativity, and motivation to pursue our goals and dreams.

However, prioritizing self-care can be challenging, especially when we are busy with work, school, or other responsibilities. It can be easy to fall into the trap of putting others' needs before our own. This is why it is important to set boundaries and make time for self-care activities that bring us joy and fulfillment. We may also need to seek support from loved ones, friends, or a mental health professional when we need it.

In summary, self-care is essential for our physical, mental, and emotional well-being. By prioritizing our own needs, we can lead happier, healthier, and more successful lives. It is important to remember that self-care is not selfish or indulgent, but rather a necessary part of maintaining our health and well-being.

CHAPTER SEVENTEEN

Patience: The Virtue of Waiting

In today's fast-paced world, waiting is often seen as a waste of time. We want everything to happen quickly, instantly, and without delay. We live in an age of instant gratification where everything is at our fingertips, and we can have it all with just a click of a button. But what if I told you that waiting is actually a virtue? That it can help you achieve greater success and happiness in both your personal and professional life? In this chapter, we will explore the concept of patience and how it can be a valuable asset in our lives.

Patience is the ability to endure waiting, delay, or provocation without becoming annoyed or upset. It is the quality of being calm, composed, and self-controlled even in the face of difficulties. Patience is not just a virtue; it is a skill that can be developed and honed over time. It requires practice and persistence, but the rewards are significant. Patience allows us to stay focused on our goals, maintain our emotional balance, and make better decisions.

In our personal lives, patience can be a key factor in building and maintaining strong relationships. It takes time to develop trust, intimacy, and understanding with others.

We need to be patient with our loved ones and give them the space and time they need to grow and change. Patience can also help us deal with difficult situations, such as illness, loss, or personal struggles. When we are patient, we are better able to cope with these challenges and come out stronger on the other side.

In our professional lives, patience can be a critical factor in achieving success. Many successful people attribute their success to their ability to stay focused, stay the course, and persevere through challenging times. Patience can help us overcome setbacks, navigate complex situations, and make better decisions. It can also help us build better relationships with our colleagues, clients, and customers. When we are patient, we are more likely to listen to others, understand their perspectives, and build stronger connections.

So how can we develop patience in our lives? Here are some strategies that can help:

- Practice mindfulness:

Mindfulness is the practice of being present and fully engaged in the current moment. It can help us develop greater awareness of our thoughts and emotions, and learn to manage them more effectively. By practicing mindfulness, we can become more patient and less reactive.

- Set realistic expectations:

Often, impatience arises when our expectations are not met. We need to learn to set realistic goals and expectations for ourselves and others. This can help us stay focused on the process rather than the outcome.

- Take a break:

Sometimes, the best way to be patient is to take a step back and give ourselves a break. Taking a walk, practicing yoga, or doing something we enjoy can help us recharge and come back to a situation with a fresh perspective.

- Practice gratitude:

Gratitude is the practice of being thankful for what we have and focusing on the positive aspects of our lives. When we practice gratitude, we are less likely to become impatient or frustrated with our circumstances.

- Learn from mistakes:

Finally, we need to learn from our mistakes and failures. These experiences can teach us valuable lessons about patience, persistence, and resilience. By embracing these lessons, we can become more patient and better equipped to handle challenges in the future.

Patience is a valuable virtue that can help us achieve greater success and happiness in our lives. It allows us to stay focused on our goals, maintain our emotional balance, and make better decisions. By practicing mindfulness, setting realistic expectations, taking a break, practicing gratitude, and learning from our mistakes, we can develop greater patience and become more resilient in the face of challenges.

Patience is an essential quality that is often overlooked in today's fast-paced society. We live in a world where everything is available at our fingertips, and we expect instant gratification. However, patience is crucial for success and happiness in both our personal and professional lives. It enables us to stay calm and composed, even in challenging situations, and make better decisions.

One of the reasons why patience is so important is that it helps us stay focused on our goals. It is easy to become distracted and lose sight of our objectives when we are constantly bombarded with distractions and interruptions. By cultivating patience, we can stay the course and persevere through difficult times, even when progress is slow.

In addition, patience helps us maintain our emotional balance. When we are impatient, we are more likely to become frustrated, angry, or anxious. These negative emotions can undermine our ability to think clearly and make rational decisions. By remaining patient, we can stay calm and level-headed, even in stressful situations.

Another benefit of patience is that it helps us build stronger relationships with others. When we are patient, we are more likely to listen to others, understand their perspectives, and show empathy. This can help us build trust, foster collaboration, and strengthen our social connections.

Developing patience is not always easy, especially in a world that values speed and efficiency. However, there are several strategies that we can use to cultivate this important virtue. For example, practicing mindfulness can help us become more aware of our thoughts and emotions, and learn to manage them more effectively. Setting realistic expectations and learning from our mistakes can also help us become more patient and resilient.

Scientific research findings that support the importance of patience:

In a study published in the Journal of Personality and Social Psychology in 2012, researchers found that individuals who were more patient tended to have better psychological and physical well-being. The study surveyed 1,000 individuals and found that those who scored higher on measures of patience reported less depression, anxiety, and stress, and also had lower levels of substance abuse.

A study published in the Journal of Positive Psychology in 2013 found that individuals who were more patient tended to be more satisfied with their lives. The study surveyed 2,400 individuals and found that those who scored higher on measures of patience reported higher levels of life satisfaction, even after controlling for other factors such as age, gender, and income.

A study published in the journal Emotion in 2016 found that individuals who were more patient tended to have better self-control. The study involved 229 participants and found that those who were more patient were better able to resist temptations, such as eating unhealthy foods or spending money impulsively.

A study published in the Journal of Positive Psychology in 2017 found that practicing mindfulness meditation can increase levels of patience. The study involved 116 participants and found that those who practiced mindfulness meditation for just 10 minutes per day for two weeks reported significantly higher levels of patience compared to a control group.

These studies demonstrate that patience is an important virtue that can have significant benefits for our well-being, satisfaction with life, self-control, and overall success. By cultivating patience through mindfulness, realistic expectations, and learning from our mistakes, we can become more resilient, better able to handle stress, and more successful in achieving our goals.

In conclusion, patience is a valuable virtue that can help us achieve greater success and happiness in our lives. It enables us to stay focused on our goals, maintain our emotional balance, and build stronger relationships with others. By cultivating patience, we can become more resilient, more empathetic, and better equipped to handle the challenges that life throws our way.

CHAPTER EIGHTEEN

Perspective: Seeing Things Differently

One of simple things that can make a huge impact in our lives is our perspective. The way we see things and interpret situations can have a significant effect on our emotions, thoughts, and actions. Our perspective can either limit us or empower us. It can either hold us back or propel us forward. Therefore, it is crucial to develop a positive and flexible perspective that can help us navigate through life's ups and downs.

The first step in developing a healthy perspective is to become aware of our current mindset. We must examine the lens through which we view the world and ourselves. Are we seeing things with a narrow or limited perspective? Do we have a fixed mindset that only focuses on what we lack, rather than what we have? Or are we seeing things with a growth mindset that focuses on possibilities and opportunities?

To change our perspective, we need to challenge our current beliefs and assumptions. We can do this by asking ourselves questions that open up new possibilities. For example, if we are feeling stuck in a particular situation, we can ask ourselves, "What would happen if I tried something new?" or "What are the benefits of stepping out of my comfort zone?" These questions can help us shift our focus from limitations to possibilities.

Another way to shift our perspective is to look at things from a different angle. We can try to see things from other people's perspectives or put ourselves in their shoes. This can help us develop empathy and compassion, which can lead to better relationships and a more positive outlook on life. We can also try to see the silver lining in difficult situations. For example, instead of focusing on the negative aspects of losing a job, we can focus on the opportunity to explore new career paths or spend more time with our loved ones.

It is also essential to develop a gratitude mindset. When we focus on what we are grateful for, we shift our attention from what we lack to what we have. We can start by making a list of things we are thankful for, no matter how small or insignificant they may seem. It could be something as simple as having a roof over our heads or a warm meal to eat. When we focus on the abundance in our lives, we attract more positivity and abundance.

Additionally, we can surround ourselves with people who have a positive and growth-oriented mindset. When we spend time with people who inspire us and challenge us to grow, we become more open-minded and receptive to new ideas and perspectives. We can also read books, listen to podcasts, or attend seminars that expose us to new ways of thinking and broaden our horizons.

Steps to implement a positive and flexible perspective:

- Journaling:

Start by reflecting on your current mindset by journaling your thoughts and feelings. This exercise can help you become aware of your limiting beliefs and thought patterns. You can also write down positive affirmations and things you are grateful for to shift your focus on the positive aspects of your life.

- Practice Empathy:

Put yourself in someone else's shoes by imagining their perspective in a situation. This exercise can help you develop empathy and understanding towards others, leading to better relationships and a more positive outlook on life.

- Question your beliefs:

Challenge your limiting beliefs and assumptions by asking yourself questions that open up new possibilities. For example, if you believe that you are not good enough for a particular job, ask yourself, "What if I applied for the job anyway? What are the benefits of trying?" This exercise can help you shift your focus from limitations to possibilities.

- Gratitude practice:

Develop a gratitude mindset by making a daily habit of writing down things you are grateful for, no matter how small or insignificant they may seem. This exercise can help you shift your attention from what you lack to what you have, leading to a more positive and abundant mindset.

- Surround yourself with positive people:

Spend time with people who inspire and challenge you to grow. This exercise can help you become more open-minded and receptive to new ideas and perspectives. You can also read books, listen to podcasts, or attend seminars that expose you to new ways of thinking and broaden your horizons.

- Shift your focus:

When you encounter a challenging situation, try to see the silver lining and focus on the positive aspects of the situation. For example, if you lose your job, focus on the opportunity to explore new career paths or spend more time with your loved ones. This exercise can help you shift your attention from the negative aspects of the situation to the opportunities and possibilities that lie ahead.

By practicing these exercises regularly, you can develop a positive and flexible perspective that empowers you and opens up new possibilities in your personal and professional life. Remember, changing your perspective is a gradual process, so be patient and kind to yourself. With time and practice, you can cultivate a perspective that helps you achieve happiness and success in life.

In conclusion, perspective is a powerful tool that can help us achieve happiness and success in life. By becoming aware of our current mindset, challenging our beliefs, looking at things from a different angle, developing a gratitude mindset, and surrounding ourselves with positive and growth-oriented people, we can cultivate a perspective that empowers us and opens up new possibilities. Remember, simple things in life, such as changing our perspective, can have the most significant impact on our lives.

CHAPTER NINETEEN

Courage: Facing Our Fears

Fear is a natural emotion that arises in response to situations or events that pose a perceived threat to our well-being or safety. It's a feeling that most of us have experienced at some point in our lives. Fear can be an overwhelming emotion, and it can cause us to avoid situations that may be necessary for personal growth and development.

However, the good news is that we have the power to overcome our fears and develop courage. Courage is not the absence of fear; rather, it's the ability to act in spite of it. In this chapter, we will explore the importance of facing our fears and developing the courage to take on new challenges.

Understanding Fear

Fear can manifest in various ways, such as anxiety, stress, or even physical symptoms like sweating, palpitations, or shortness of breath. However, it's essential to understand that fear is a natural response to situations that our brains perceive as a threat. It's a survival mechanism that has helped humans survive and evolve over time.

Fear can be categorized into two types - rational and irrational. Rational fear is based on a realistic threat, such as being afraid of snakes or heights. However, irrational fear is a response to a situation that is not necessarily dangerous, such as public speaking or meeting new people.

Overcoming Fear

Fear can hold us back from achieving our full potential. It can prevent us from taking on new challenges, trying new experiences, or pursuing our dreams. However, the good news is that we have the power to overcome our fears.

The first step in overcoming fear is to acknowledge it. We need to identify the source of our fear and understand why we feel that way. Once we understand our fears, we can start working towards overcoming them.

One effective way to overcome fear is through exposure therapy. Exposure therapy involves gradually exposing ourselves to situations or events that trigger our fears. For example, if we are afraid of public speaking, we can start by speaking in front of a small group of people and gradually work our way up to larger audiences.

Another way to overcome fear is to reframe our thoughts. We need to challenge our negative thoughts and beliefs that are holding us back. Instead of thinking, "I can't do it," we can reframe our thoughts to "I can do it, and I will succeed."

Developing Courage

Courage is the ability to face our fears and take action in spite of them. It's not something that comes naturally to everyone, but it's a skill that can be developed through practice.

One way to develop courage is through self-reflection. We need to take the time to understand our values, beliefs, and goals. Once we know what's important to us, we can start taking action towards our goals, even if it means facing our fears.

Another way to develop courage is through positive self-talk. We need to talk to ourselves in an encouraging and supportive manner. We need to remind ourselves that we are capable of achieving our goals and that we have the skills and abilities to overcome any obstacles that come our way.

Finally, we need to surround ourselves with people who support and encourage us. We need to build a support network of family, friends, and mentors who can provide us with guidance and encouragement when we need it.

Fear is a natural emotion that we all experience, but it shouldn't hold us back from achieving our full potential. We need to acknowledge our fears, challenge our negative thoughts, and take action towards our goals, even if it means facing our fears.

Developing courage is not an easy task, but it's essential for personal growth and development. We can develop courage through self-reflection, positive self-talk, and building a support network of people who encourage and support us.

Remember, courage is not the absence of fear, but the ability to act in spite of it. It's a skill that can be developed and honed through practice and perseverance. By facing our fears and taking action towards our goals, we can overcome our limitations and achieve success in both our personal and professional lives.

Moreover, it's important to keep in mind that courage is not a one-time thing. It's a continuous process that requires ongoing effort and dedication. We may face new fears and challenges throughout our lives, but by developing the courage to face them, we can continue to grow and evolve as individuals.

There is ample research on the benefits of facing fears and developing courage. Here are a few examples:

A study published in the Journal of Positive Psychology found that individuals who actively faced their fears experienced a greater sense of well-being and life satisfaction than those who avoided their fears (Watt & Stewart, 2013).

In another study published in the Journal of Experimental Psychology, participants who faced their fears and took action towards their goals experienced an increase in self-confidence and motivation (Gollwitzer & Sheeran, 2006).

A 2015 study published in the Journal of Personality and Social Psychology found that individuals who had developed courage and resilience were more likely to overcome traumatic events and bounce back from adversity (Southwick & Charney, 2015).

A 2016 study published in the Journal of Career Development found that individuals who faced their fears and took on new challenges in the workplace experienced greater job satisfaction and career success (Moloney & Hurrell, 2016).

According to a 2019 survey conducted by the American Psychological Association, individuals who faced their fears and took action towards their goals reported higher levels of well-being and lower levels of stress than those who did not (APA, 2019).

These studies demonstrate the importance of facing fears and developing courage in both personal and professional settings. By taking action towards our goals, we can increase our sense of well-being, self-confidence, and motivation, and overcome adversity when it arises.

In the end, simple things in life often require the most courage. Whether it's starting a new job, asking someone out on a date, or pursuing a passion project, it takes courage to step outside our comfort zones and take risks. But by facing our fears and developing the courage to take action, we can unlock our full potential and live a fulfilling life.

So, the next time you're faced with a challenging situation or a new opportunity, remember that you have the power to overcome your fears and develop the courage to take on whatever comes your way. Embrace the challenges, learn from your experiences, and keep moving forward with courage and confidence.

CHAPTER TWENTY

Resilience: Bouncing Back from Adversity

Life is full of ups and downs, and we all experience setbacks at some point in our lives. It could be losing a job, ending a relationship, or facing a health crisis. While these challenges can be overwhelming and daunting, they also present opportunities for growth and self-discovery. Resilience is the ability to bounce back from adversity, to withstand difficult times, and emerge stronger and more adaptable. In this chapter, we'll explore the concept of resilience, and how you can cultivate it to navigate life's challenges.

What is Resilience?

Resilience is the capacity to adapt and recover from adversity, trauma, or stress. It is not a fixed trait, but rather a dynamic process that can be developed and strengthened over time. Resilient individuals possess a set of attitudes and behaviours that enable them to cope with difficult situations and bounce back from setbacks. These include:

- Optimism:

Resilient individuals maintain a positive outlook, even in the face of adversity. They view setbacks as temporary, and believe they can overcome them.

- Flexibility:

Resilient individuals are adaptable and able to adjust to changing circumstances. They are open to new perspectives and approaches, and are willing to try different strategies.

- Self-efficacy:

Resilient individuals have a strong sense of self-efficacy, or belief in their ability to succeed. They are confident in their skills and abilities, and are willing to take on challenges.

- Social support:

Resilient individuals have a network of supportive relationships that provide emotional, informational, and practical support during difficult times. They seek out and maintain strong connections with family, friends, and colleagues.

- Coping skills:

Resilient individuals have developed effective coping skills that enable them to manage stress and regulate their emotions. They may use techniques such as mindfulness, meditation, exercise, or therapy.

Why is Resilience Important?

Resilience is important for several reasons. Firstly, it helps us cope with adversity and stress, which are inevitable parts of life. By developing resilience, we can better manage difficult situations and maintain our emotional wellbeing. also, resilience enables us to adapt to change and navigate transitions. In today's fast-paced and rapidly changing world, the ability to adapt is essential for success. Resilience fosters personal growth and development. By overcoming challenges and setbacks, we can develop new skills, perspectives, and strengths that can benefit us in all areas of life.

How to Develop Resilience

Resilience is a skill that can be developed and strengthened over time. Here are some strategies you can use to cultivate resilience:

- Practice optimism:

Cultivate a positive outlook and focus on the opportunities for growth and learning that arise from adversity. Use positive self-talk to reframe negative thoughts and beliefs.

- Build relationships:

Develop strong connections with family, friends, and colleagues. Seek out social support when you need it, and offer support to others in turn.

- Develop coping skills:

Learn and practice effective coping skills such as mindfulness, meditation, exercise, or therapy. Experiment with different techniques to find what works best for you.

- Take care of yourself:

Prioritize self-care activities that promote physical, emotional, and mental wellbeing. Get enough sleep, eat a healthy diet, and engage in activities that bring you joy and fulfillment.

- Learn from setbacks:

View setbacks as opportunities for learning and growth. Reflect on what went wrong and what you can do differently next time.

- Set goals:

Set realistic goals for yourself, and break them down into smaller, achievable steps. Celebrate your successes along the way, and learn from any setbacks or challenges.

- Embrace change:

Practice flexibility and adaptability. Be open to new perspectives and approaches, and be willing to try different strategies.

- Develop a sense of purpose:

Identify your values and goals, and work towards them with intention and purpose. Having a sense of purpose can provide motivation and direction during difficult times.

- Practice gratitude:

Cultivate a sense of gratitude for the good things in your life, even in the midst of adversity. Express gratitude to others, and take time to appreciate the small moments of joy and beauty around you.

- Seek professional help:

If you are struggling with difficult emotions or mental health issues, seek professional help from a therapist or counsellor. They can provide support and guidance as you navigate difficult times.

Resilience is a vital skill for navigating life's challenges and bouncing back from adversity. By cultivating a positive outlook, building strong relationships, developing coping skills, and taking care of ourselves, we can develop resilience and adapt to changing circumstances. Remember, resilience is not a fixed trait, but a dynamic process that can be developed and strengthened over time. With practice and determination, we can overcome setbacks and emerge stronger and more resilient than before.

CHAPTER TWENTY-ONE

Mindset: The Power of Positive Thinking

The human mind is a powerful tool that can shape our lives. Our thoughts, beliefs, and attitudes can determine how we perceive the world, how we react to challenges, and ultimately, the kind of life we lead. This is where the concept of mindset comes into play. Your mindset is your mental attitude or inclination, and it influences the way you think and act. In this chapter, we will explore the power of positive thinking and how it can transform your life.

What is Positive Thinking?

Positive thinking is a mental attitude that focuses on the positive aspects of life, while minimizing or eliminating the negative ones. It is the practice of looking at the bright side of things and finding the silver lining in every situation. Positive thinking doesn't mean ignoring or denying the negative aspects of life; it means choosing to focus on the good rather than the bad.

Positive thinking is not a magical solution that can solve all your problems overnight. However, it can help you develop a more optimistic and resilient mindset, which can help you cope better with stress, setbacks, and challenges. A positive mindset can also enhance your creativity, boost your confidence, and improve your relationships.

The Power of Positive Thinking

Positive thinking has been the subject of numerous studies, and the findings suggest that it can have a significant impact on our lives. One of the most famous studies in this field is the "Pygmalion effect" study conducted by psychologist Robert Rosenthal and Lenore Jacobson in 1968. In this study, they found that teachers who were told that certain students had high potential (regardless of their actual ability) treated them differently, resulting in higher academic performance for those students. This study demonstrated that our expectations and beliefs about ourselves and others can shape our reality.

Similarly, a study published in the Journal of Personality and Social Psychology found that individuals who maintained a positive mindset experienced better health outcome and lived longer than those with a negative mindset. Another study conducted at the University of Pennsylvania found that optimistic salespeople outsold their pessimistic counterparts by 56%.

These studies illustrate the power of positive thinking and how it can impact various aspects of our lives, including health, relationships, and success.

How to Develop a Positive Mindset

Developing a positive mindset takes time and effort, but it is a worthwhile investment in your overall well-being.

Here are some tips to help you cultivate a positive mindset:

- Practice Gratitude:

Gratitude is the practice of appreciating the good things in your life. It can help you focus on the positive aspects of your life and minimize the negative ones. One way to cultivate gratitude is to keep a gratitude journal, where you write down three things you are grateful for each day. This simple practice can help shift your focus from what you lack to what you have.

- Challenge Negative Thoughts:

Negative thoughts can sabotage your efforts to develop a positive mindset. When you notice negative thoughts creeping in, challenge them by questioning their validity. Ask yourself if they are based on facts or assumptions. If they are assumptions, try to reframe them in a more positive light.

- Surround Yourself with Positive People:

The people you surround yourself with can have a significant impact on your mindset. Surround yourself with positive, supportive people who lift you up and encourage you to grow. Avoid people who are negative, critical, or constantly bring you down.

- Celebrate Small Wins:

It's easy to get caught up in the pursuit of big goals and forget to celebrate the small wins along the way.

Celebrating small wins can help you maintain a positive mindset and build momentum towards achieving your larger goals. Take time to acknowledge and celebrate your achievements, no matter how small they may seem.

- Reframe Negative Experiences:

Negative experiences are a part of life, but how you perceive and react to them can make all the difference. Try reframing negative experiences in a more positive light. Look for the lessons you can learn from them or the opportunities they present for growth.

- Focus on Solutions, Not Problems:

When faced with challenges, it's easy to get bogged down by the problems at hand. Instead of focusing solely on the problems, shift your focus to finding solutions. This can help you maintain a positive mindset and feel more empowered to overcome obstacles.

Here are scientific research studies that support the power of positive thinking:

In a study published in the Journal of Personality and Social Psychology in 1995, researchers found that participants who were primed with positive words were more likely to perceive neutral stimuli as positive than those who were primed with negative or neutral words.

A 2000 study published in the Journal of Social and Clinical Psychology found that optimism was associated with lower levels of anxiety and depression in college students.

In a 2003 study published in the Journal of Psychosomatic Research, researchers found that optimism was associated with better immune function in elderly patients with chronic obstructive pulmonary disease.

A 2004 study published in the Journal of Personality and Social Psychology found that individuals who wrote about positive experiences for 20 minutes a day for three consecutive days had improved mood and fewer health complaints compared to those who wrote about negative experiences.

In a 2006 study published in the Journal of Health Psychology, researchers found that optimism was associated with better quality of life and fewer physical symptoms in individuals with multiple sclerosis.

A 2007 study published in the Journal of Personality and Social Psychology found that individuals who were primed with positive words were more likely to engage in prosocial behaviour than those who were primed with negative words.

In a 2009 study published in the Journal of Positive Psychology, researchers found that individuals who practiced gratitude for two weeks had increased happiness and life satisfaction compared to a control group.

A 2010 study published in the Journal of Personality and Social Psychology found that individuals who were primed with positive words were more likely to solve problems creatively than those who were primed with negative words.

In a 2012 study published in the Journal of Experimental Social Psychology, researchers found that individuals who were primed with positive words were more likely to trust others and cooperate in a social dilemma game than those who were primed with negative words.

A 2013 study published in the Journal of Abnormal Psychology found that individuals who had a positive cognitive style had lower levels of depression and anxiety than those with a negative cognitive style.

In a 2014 study published in the Journal of Experimental Psychology: General, researchers found that individuals who practiced mindfulness for eight weeks had improved working memory capacity compared to a control group.

A 2015 study published in the Journal of Social Psychology found that individuals who practiced self-compassion had improved well-being and reduced symptoms of depression and anxiety.

In a 2016 study published in the Journal of Applied Psychology, researchers found that employees who had a positive outlook had higher job satisfaction and were less likely to experience burnout.

A 2018 study published in the Journal of Happiness Studies found that individuals who practiced kindness towards others had increased happiness and life satisfaction compared to a control group.

In a 2020 study published in the Journal of Personality and Social Psychology, researchers found that individuals who engaged in positive self-talk had improved mood and reduced stress levels compared to those who engaged in negative self-talk.

A positive mindset is a powerful tool that can transform your life. By focusing on the positive aspects of life, challenging negative thoughts, surrounding yourself with positive people, practicing mindfulness, celebrating small wins, reframing negative experiences, and focusing on solutions, you can cultivate a more positive mindset and improve your overall well-being. Remember, developing a positive mindset takes time and effort, but it is a worthwhile investment in your personal and professional growth. Embrace the power of positive thinking and watch your life transform.

CHAPTER TWENTY-TWO

Purpose: Finding Meaning in Life

Introduction:

In this chapter, we will discuss the importance of finding a purpose or meaning in life. Many of us go through our lives without a clear understanding of our purpose, and this can lead to a feeling of emptiness or lack of direction. However, when we find our purpose, it can bring a sense of fulfillment and satisfaction that can greatly enhance our personal and professional lives.

What is Purpose?

Purpose is the reason for which something is done or created, or for which something exists. It is a sense of direction, a driving force that gives meaning to our lives. Without a purpose, we may feel lost or unfulfilled, as if we are merely going through the motions of life without any real direction or meaning.

Why is Purpose Important?

Having a clear sense of purpose is essential for our overall well-being. It provides us with a sense of direction, motivates us to take action, and helps us to stay focused and committed to our goals. Purpose gives us a reason to wake up in the morning, to work hard and strive for success. It can also help us to overcome obstacles and challenges, as we have a clear sense of what we are working towards.

How to Find Your Purpose:

Finding your purpose is a process that can take time, and it often involves a great deal of self-reflection and exploration. Here are some steps that you can take to help you find your purpose:

- Identify Your Passions:

Think about the things that you enjoy doing the most. What are your hobbies, interests, and talents? What activities bring you the most joy and fulfillment? Identifying your passions can help you to understand what you are naturally drawn to, and can help to guide you towards a purpose that aligns with your values and goals.

- Consider Your Values:

Think about the things that are most important to you in life. What do you value the most? Is it family, community, spirituality, or something else? Understanding your values can help you to identify a purpose that aligns with your beliefs and principles.

- Reflect on Your Strengths and Weaknesses:

Consider your personal strengths and weaknesses. What are you good at, and what challenges you? Understanding your strengths and weaknesses can help you to identify opportunities for personal growth, and can help you to find a purpose that allows you to utilize your strengths to their fullest potential.

- Explore Different Career Paths:

If you are unsure about your purpose, consider exploring different career paths. This can help you to gain experience and exposure to different industries and roles, and can help you to identify your strengths and passions.

- Seek Inspiration:

Look for inspiration in the world around you. Read books, attend lectures and events, and talk to people who inspire you. Seeking inspiration can help you to gain clarity and focus, and can help you to identify a purpose that resonates with you.

Benefits of Finding Your Purpose

When you find your purpose, it can bring many benefits to your personal and professional life. Here are just a few of the ways that finding your purpose can enhance your life:

- Increased Fulfillment:

When you have a clear sense of purpose, you are more likely to feel fulfilled and satisfied with your life. You have a reason for getting up in the morning, and you are working towards something that is meaningful to you.

- Greater Resilience:

Having a purpose can help you to be more resilient in the face of challenges and setbacks. You have a clear sense of what you are working towards, and this can help you to stay motivated and focused, even when things get tough.

- Improved Well-being:

Research has shown that people who have a sense of purpose are more likely to have better mental and physical health. Having a purpose can provide a sense of meaning and direction in life, which can lead to improved overall well-being.

- Increased Productivity:

When you have a clear sense of purpose, you are more likely to be productive and motivated. You have a reason to work hard and strive for success, and this can help you to stay focused and committed to your goals.

- Greater Sense of Community:
- When you find your purpose, you are more likely to connect with others who share your passions and values. This can help to create a sense of community and belonging, which can enhance your personal and professional life.

In conclusion, finding your purpose is an essential part of living a fulfilling and successful life. It provides a sense of direction, motivates us to take action, and helps us to stay focused and committed to our goals. While finding your purpose can take time and effort, it is a worthwhile endeavour that can bring many benefits to your personal and professional life. By identifying your passions, values, strengths, and weaknesses, and seeking inspiration from the world around you, you can discover a purpose that aligns with your goals and values, and bring meaning and fulfillment to your life.

CHAPTER TWENTY-THREE

Service: Helping Others

There is a great joy in helping others. In fact, it can be said that true happiness and success come from helping others. It is a simple act that has the power to transform lives, both of those who receive the help and of those who give it. In this chapter, we will explore the many benefits of service and how it can change our lives and the lives of those around us.

Why Help Others?

The act of helping others is a fundamental aspect of human nature. We have an innate desire to make a difference in the world and to contribute to the well-being of others. When we help others, we feel good about ourselves and the impact we have made on the world. It is an act of kindness that is contagious and has the potential to inspire others to do the same.

Moreover, helping others can also provide a sense of purpose and meaning in life. It can help us feel connected to something bigger than ourselves and give us a sense of fulfillment that cannot be found in material possessions or personal achievements.

The Benefits of Helping Others

There are many benefits to helping others, both for the recipient of the help and for the giver. Some of the most significant benefits include:

- Improved Mental Health:

Helping others has been linked to reduced levels of depression and anxiety. It can also improve self-esteem and provide a sense of purpose and meaning in life.

- Stronger Communities:

When individuals come together to help one another, it strengthens the bonds within the community. This, in turn, leads to more cooperation and collaboration, and a greater sense of unity and belonging.

- Personal Growth:

Helping others requires us to step outside of our comfort zones and develop new skills and perspectives. It can also help us to develop empathy and compassion, which are essential qualities for personal growth and development.

- Improved Relationships:

When we help others, we build trust and respect with those around us. This can lead to deeper and more meaningful relationships with friends, family, and colleagues.

- Better Physical Health:

There is evidence to suggest that helping others can improve physical health. This may be due to the reduced stress and increased social support that comes with helping others.

Ways to Help Others

There are many ways to help others, and it doesn't have to be a grand gesture to make a difference. Some simple ways to help others include:

- Volunteering:

Volunteering your time and skills is a great way to make a difference in your community. Whether it's at a local food bank, hospital, or school, there are many opportunities to give back.

- Random Acts of Kindness:

Doing small things for others can have a big impact. This could include buying someone a coffee, holding the door open for someone, or simply smiling at a stranger.

- Donating:

Donating to a charity or cause that you care about is a great way to support others. This could include donating money, goods, or services.

- Mentoring:

Mentoring someone can be a powerful way to make a difference in their life. Whether it's a young person or someone starting a new career, your guidance and support can have a significant impact.

Supporting a Friend or Family Member: Sometimes, the best way to help someone is to simply be there for them. This could include listening, offering words of encouragement, or helping them with a task or project.

Service is an essential aspect of human nature, and helping others is a simple yet powerful way to make a difference in the world. Whether it's through volunteering, donating, mentoring, or simply being there for someone, the act of helping others has the potential to transform lives and bring joy and fulfillment to our own. By embracing service, we can build stronger communities, improve our mental and physical health, and develop important qualities like empathy and compassion. In a world that can often be overwhelming and stressful, helping others is a way to find purpose and meaning in our lives, while also making a positive impact on the world around us.

It's important to note that while helping others can be incredibly rewarding, it's not always easy. It can be challenging to step outside of our comfort zones and offer our time and resources to others. It's important to acknowledge that and to be kind to ourselves in the process.

It's also important to recognize that service doesn't have to be a one-time event or a grand gesture. Small acts of kindness can have just as much of an impact as larger ones. By making service a part of our daily lives, we can create a ripple effect of kindness and positivity in the world.

In conclusion, service and helping others are fundamental aspects of human nature that have the power to transform lives and communities. By embracing service, we can find purpose and meaning in our lives, improve our mental and physical health, and develop important qualities like empathy and compassion. Whether it's through volunteering, donating, mentoring, or simply being there for someone, there are countless ways to make a difference in the world. By making service a part of our daily lives, we can create a more compassionate and connected world, one small act of kindness at a time.

CHAPTER TWENTY-FOUR

Simplicity in the Workplace: Achieving Success with Less

In today's fast-paced and constantly changing work environment, it's easy to get lost in the chaos of endless meetings, deadlines, and to-do lists. The pressure to be productive and efficient can sometimes make us overlook the power of simplicity. However, embracing simplicity in the workplace can actually help us achieve success with less stress and more ease. In this chapter, we will explore the benefits of simplicity in the workplace and how to implement it in your daily routine.

Benefits of simplicity in the workplace:

- Increased productivity:

Simplifying your work routine can help you focus on the most important tasks and complete them efficiently, which ultimately leads to increased productivity. When your work environment and tasks are simplified, you can spend less time trying to figure out what to do next and more time actually getting work done. This can help you meet your goals more quickly and effectively.

- Improved clarity and decision-making:

Simplifying your work routine can help improve clarity and decision-making by reducing confusion and distractions. When your tasks and goals are clearly defined, you can make better decisions about how to prioritize your time and efforts. This can help you avoid wasting time on tasks that aren't important and focus on what really matters.

- Reduced stress and burnout:

Simplifying your work routine can help reduce stress and burnout by eliminating unnecessary tasks and creating a more manageable workload. When you're not overwhelmed by too many tasks or distractions, you can feel more in control of your work and less likely to become burnt out. This can lead to increased job satisfaction and better overall well-being.

- Enhanced creativity and innovation:

Simplifying your work routine can free up mental space, allowing you to be more creative and innovative in your work. When you're not bogged down by unnecessary tasks or distractions, you can have more mental energy to focus on problem-solving and coming up with new ideas. This can lead to more innovative solutions and better results.

How to implement simplicity in the workplace:

- Streamline your workspace:

Start by decluttering your workspace and organizing your files and documents. Keep only what you need and eliminate any unnecessary items or distractions. A clutter-free workspace can help you stay focused and feel more organized.

- Prioritize your tasks:

Create a list of your daily tasks and prioritize them based on their importance and urgency. This will help you focus on the most important tasks first and avoid getting bogged down by less important ones. This can help you make the most of your time and be more productive.

- Simplify your communication:

Avoid overcomplicating communication with colleagues and clients. Use simple and concise language to ensure everyone is on the same page. This can help avoid misunderstandings and make communication more efficient.

- Limit meetings:

Meetings can often be a waste of time and a drain on productivity. Limit the number of meetings you attend and ensure they are necessary and productive. This can help you free up time to focus on your work and stay on track with your goals.

- Embrace technology:

Use technology to your advantage by automating repetitive tasks and utilizing tools that simplify your work routine. This can help you be more efficient and save time that can be spent on more important tasks.

Examples of simplicity in the workplace:

- Apple: Apple is known for its simple and intuitive product design, which has helped make them a global leader in technology. By simplifying their products, they have created a user-friendly experience that sets them apart from their competitors. Apple's commitment to simplicity has helped them create a loyal customer base and achieve great success.

- Google: Google's search engine is a prime example of simplicity in action. By keeping their homepage clean and uncluttered, they have created a user-friendly experience that is easy to navigate and use. This simplicity has helped make Google one of the most popular search engines in the world.

- IngiGo Airlines: IndiGoAirlines has a simple business model that focuses on providing low-cost flights with exceptional customer service. By keeping their business model simple, they have been able to successfully compete with larger airlines. This simplicity has helped them build a loyal customer base and achieve financial success.

- IKEA: IKEA is known for its simple and affordable furniture designs. By focusing on simplicity and functionality, they have created a unique and recognizable brand that appeals to a wide range of customers. IKEA's commitment to simplicity has helped them become one of the largest furniture retailers in the world.

- Basecamp: Basecamp is a project management software that prides itself on its simplicity. By offering a streamlined interface and essential features, they have created a software that is easy to use and navigate. Basecamp's commitment to simplicity has helped them build a loyal user base and achieve success in a crowded market.

Simplicity in the workplace can lead to increased productivity, improved decision-making, reduced stress and burnout, and enhanced creativity and innovation. To implement simplicity in the workplace, streamline your workspace, prioritize your tasks, simplify your communication, limit meetings, and embrace technology. By embracing simplicity, you can achieve success with less and enjoy a more fulfilling and satisfying work life.

CHAPTER TWENTY-FIVE

Living a Simple, Successful Life

In today's world, we often get caught up in the hustle and bustle of daily life. We are constantly on the go, working long hours, and trying to keep up with the latest trends and technology. In the midst of all this chaos, we often forget the simple things that can bring us joy and fulfillment.

This is where the concept of living a simple, successful life comes in. By focusing on the small things that matter most, we can create a life that is both fulfilling and successful. In this final chapter, we will explore some of the key principles of living a simple, successful life and how you can apply them in your own life.

Appreciating the Simple Things

The first principle of living a simple life is to appreciate the simple things. This means taking time to enjoy the small moments that make life worthwhile. It could be something as simple as a quiet moment alone, a beautiful sunset, or a warm hug from a loved one. These small moments may seem insignificant, but they can bring us immense joy and happiness.

To appreciate the simple things, you must first learn to slow down and be present in the moment. This means putting aside distractions and focusing on the here and now. When you are fully present, you can better appreciate the small things that make life so special.

Simplicity in Daily Life

The second principle of living a simple life is to simplify your daily life. This means eliminating the excess clutter and distractions that can weigh you down and prevent you from reaching your full potential. Simplifying your life could mean decluttering your home, minimizing your possessions, or simplifying your daily routine.

When you simplify your life, you free up mental and physical space to focus on what truly matters. You can then direct your energy towards your goals and passions, and achieve greater success in all areas of your life.

Living in the Moment

The third principle of living a simple, successful life is to live in the moment. This means letting go of the past and not worrying about the future. When you are fully present in the moment, you can enjoy life to the fullest and make the most of every opportunity.

Living in the moment also means being grateful for what you have right now. Instead of always wanting more, take time to appreciate what you already have. This gratitude will bring you a greater sense of joy and contentment in your daily life.

Balancing Work and Play

The fourth principle of living a simple, successful life is to find balance between work and play. Many of us get caught up in our work and forget to take time for ourselves and our loved ones. However, it is essential to find a healthy balance between work and play in order to live a happy and fulfilling life.

When you take time for yourself and your loved ones, you recharge your batteries and come back to work with renewed energy and focus. This allows you to be more productive and successful in your career, while still enjoying a fulfilling personal life.

Creating Meaningful Relationships

The final principle of living a simple, successful life is to create meaningful relationships. Humans are social creatures, and we thrive on connection and community. By cultivating meaningful relationships with others, we can find support, inspiration, and a sense of belonging.

To create meaningful relationships, you must be willing to invest time and energy into building and maintaining them. This could mean reaching out to old friends, joining a new social group, or simply being more present in your current relationships.

Conclusion

Living a simple, successful life is not about achieving perfection or accumulating wealth and possessions. It is about appreciating the simple things, simplifying your daily life, living in the moment, balancing work and play, and creating meaningful relationships. By focusing on these principles, you can create a life that is fulfilling, joyful, and successful.

It is important to note that living a simple, successful life is not a one-time event or a destination. Rather, it is an ongoing journey that requires constant attention and effort. You will encounter challenges and setbacks along the way, but by staying true to these principles, you can overcome them and continue to grow and thrive.

Remember that living a simple, successful life is a personal journey that is unique to each individual. What works for one person may not work for another, and that is okay. The key is to find what resonates with you and make it a part of your daily life.

In closing, I hope that this book has inspired you to embrace the simple things in life and live a life that is both simple and successful. By focusing on what truly matters and letting go of the excess, you can create a life that is full of joy, purpose, and fulfillment.

www.ingramcontent.com/pod-product-compliance
Lightning Source LLC
LaVergne TN
LVHW021155160826
845679LV00024B/2131

* 9 7 9 8 8 9 1 3 3 0 4 0 5 *